AF408427

THE ULTIMATE GUIDE TO WRITING WITH CHAT GPT

HARNESS THE POWER OF CHAT GPT TO WRITE SMARTER, NOT HARDER

ALEX G ZARATE

Other books written by Alex G Zarate:

Urban Fantasy/Supernatural Suspense:

Linked
Ripples of Mind
Echoes of Innocence
Connections In Crimson
Reflections In Darkness
Tremors In Time

Science Fiction:

Drake's Orb

Non-Fiction:

Zarate Zen: Captured Images From My Life To Yours
Zarate Zen: Colorful Captures & Positive Posts

The Ultimate Guide to Writing With Chat GPT: Harness The Power
Of Chat GPT To Write Smarter, Not Harder

THE ULTIMATE GUIDE TO WRITING WITH CHAT GPT:

Harness The Power Of ChatGPT To Write Smarter, Not Harder

Alex G Zarate

Disclaimer: The Ultimate Guide To Writing With Chat GPT is intended for informational and educational purposes only. The valuable insights and data provided in this book are designed to empower authors on their creative journey, guiding them to enhance their craft and overcome the hurdles on the path to publication.

With a spirit of encouragement, this book aims to inspire writers. It emphasizes that the tools needed for growth and inspiration are readily available, serving as a beacon of hope to those seeking to unlock their full creative potential.

Let this guide be your compass, pointing you towards new horizons in the realm of writing, and empowering you to weave stories that resonate with readers. May your journey be filled with discovery, growth, and endless inspiration!

This book is dedicated to every writer
struggling to find the tools needed for success.

Never stop adding to your knowledge, skills
and passion for the written word.

Keep Creating.
Keep Dreaming.

Onwards! +

Contents

INTRODUCTION
Why ChatGPT Is An Essential Tool For Authors

As a language model trained by OpenAI, ChatGPT has the ability to generate human-like responses to various prompts and inquiries.

ChatGPT's capabilities include language translation, chatbot services, and text generation. However, it can be particularly helpful in assisting authors with their writing.

Writing can be a challenging and time-consuming process. Authors must not only develop compelling characters, plotlines, and settings, but they must also ensure that their writing is grammatically correct, structurally sound, and stylistically appropriate. This can be a daunting task, even for the most experienced writers.

That's where ChatGPT comes in. As a language model, ChatGPT can help with a variety of tasks. For example, ChatGPT can help with brainstorming ideas for plotlines, character development, and editing. it can also help authors fine-tune their writing by providing suggestions for sentence structure, word choice, and overall clarity.

ChatGPT can be an invaluable resource for authors who are struggling with writer's block or who are simply looking for inspiration. It can generate writing prompts and offer guidance on how to develop a unique voice and style.

One of the most significant benefits is the ability to save time. Writing can be a time-consuming process and many authors don't have the luxury of spending hours (or days) crafting the perfect sentence or paragraph. With assistance, authors can focus on the creative side of writing. ChatGPT can take care of the technical side.

ChatGPT can also provide a level of consistency to an author's writing. As a resource, ChatGPT helps authors ensure their writing is grammatically correct, structurally sound, and stylistically appropriate. This is especially helpful when writing a series of books.

The benefits of using ChatGPT are many. As a tool, it can save authors time, providing guidance, inspiration, and help with improving the quality of our writing. As authors, it is important to utilize all available services as we embark on our writing adventures.

Onwards! +

1
STARTING
How Use ChatGPT

Congratulations on taking the first step towards becoming a better author with ChatGPT! As an AI language model trained by OpenAI, ChatGPT is a powerful tool that can help unlock new avenues of creative expression and bring your ideas to life.

We are all familiar with the autocorrect feature in our phones. It can be a great tool to write faster messages or use spell check on the go. Features like spellcheck, autocorrect and artificial intelligence assistants like Siri, Alexa and Cortana, over time, can become the most useful tools at our disposal. Each are made to assist us in different ways and as long as we understand what they can do, each one gives us the right help when we need it.

The same can be said for ChatGPT.

As defined, ChatGPT is a language model Artificial Intelligence. Meaning, it responds to you as if it were a person. Once you create an account and log in, you can jump in and ask it for answers that are not so easy to obtain when using typical search engines. For example, if you ask ChatGPT to give you a recipe for homemade chicken soup:

Q: Please provide a recipe for homemade chicken soup.

A: Certainly! Here's a recipe for homemade chicken soup:
Ingredients:
1 whole chicken (about 4 pounds)
10 cups water
2 carrots, peeled and chopped
2 celery stalks, chopped
1 onion, chopped
3 cloves garlic, minced
1 bay leaf
1 teaspoon dried thyme
1 teaspoon dried rosemary
Salt and pepper to taste
1 cup wide egg noodles (optional)
Fresh parsley, chopped (for garnish)

Instructions:
Place the whole chicken in a large pot and pour in the water. Bring it to a boil over high heat, then reduce the heat to low and let it simmer for about 1 hour, or until the chicken is cooked through and tender.

Carefully remove the chicken from the pot and set it aside to cool. Once it's cool enough to handle, shred the meat into bite-sized pieces and discard the skin and bones.

Skim any excess fat from the surface of the broth in the pot. Add the chopped carrots, celery, onion, garlic, bay leaf, thyme, and rosemary. Season with salt and pepper to taste.

Bring the soup back to a simmer and cook for about 20-30 minutes, or until the vegetables are tender.

If desired, add the egg noodles to the soup and cook for an additional 8-10 minutes, or until the noodles are cooked al dente.

Return the shredded chicken to the pot and stir well to combine. Cook for another 5 minutes to heat the chicken through.

Taste the soup and adjust the seasoning if needed. Remove the bay leaf before serving.

Ladle the homemade chicken soup into bowls and garnish with freshly chopped parsley.

Enjoy your homemade chicken soup!

Once you have your answer, you can continue asking as if texting a real person, modifying as needed. Ask ChatGPT to make the recipe Vegan, Paleo or Keto. Treat the chat like you would if a master chef were on the other side of your screen.

Trying the same thing on a typical search engine would produce a response filled with site links, articles and blogs that may touch on the topic you asked about… along with an array of ads.

Asking questions using search engines has been (for the most part) a long journey of multiple-choice juggling.

Getting started with ChatGPT as an author may seem daunting at first, but with a little guidance and practice, you can wield this revolutionary tool like a pro. Whether you're a seasoned writer or just starting out, ChatGPT can provide a wealth of inspiration, guidance, and feedback to help you hone your craft and achieve your goals. Here are some quick tips to help get you started:

FAMILIARIZE YOURSELF WITH CHATGPT.

Before we dive into writing options, read the documentation and FAQs provided by OpenAI. This gives an overview of what ChatGPT can do, how to use it, and how to get the most out of this remarkable AI tool. Take your time to Explore ChatGPT's features and capabilities. ChatGPT is capable of generating a wide range of content.

It's recommended to begin by asking easy questions or giving it simple prompts to generate responses. This will help you understand how ChatGPT responds and what types of answers you can expect.

From short stories and poems to essays and articles, ChatGPT can provide the assistance needed to cut down on time, improve quality and increase productivity. You can even use ChatGPT to help with research or brainstorming ideas.

Also, ChatGPT has various settings that can be adjusted to customize your experience. Try experimenting with these settings to see how they affect ChatGPT's responses and to find the ones that work best for you. When you understand what ChatGPT can do, you'll be able to use it more effectively and get better results.

PRACTICE, PRACTICE, PRACTICE

The more you use ChatGPT, the better it will work for you and the more familiar you will become with its features and capabilities. Practice as you go and try different types of queries and prompts to get the most out of the platform.

A quick tip to think about: Don't use it like a search engine and type a title or a web site as an inquiry. As stated above, ChatGPT is made for conversations. You can spend hours chatting with this AI, (if you so desire). Rather than looking for search results that a typical search engine uses, begin by either asking or telling ChatGPT what you want, like:

Q: What are the best available podcasts for authors?

ChatGPT will immediately give you results that you can use, rather than a line of links to articles that ask similar questions.

When I entered the question, I got the following response:

A: There are many great podcasts available for authors, but here are some of the most popular and highly recommended ones:

Writing Excuses: Hosted by Brandon Sanderson, Mary Robinette Kowal, Dan Wells, and Howard Tayler, this podcast covers a wide range of topics related to writing, from the craft of writing to the business of publishing.

The Creative Penn Podcast: Hosted by Joanna Penn, this podcast features interviews with successful authors and publishing experts, as well as advice and tips on writing, marketing, and self-publishing.

The Author Hangout: Hosted by Shawn Manaher, this podcast offers practical advice and tips on writing, publishing, and marketing your book.

The Self-Publishing Show: Hosted by Mark Dawson and James Blatch, this podcast is focused on self-publishing, offering advice and tips on everything from writing to marketing your book.

The Writer's Digest Podcast: Hosted by Gabriela Pereira, this podcast features interviews with authors and publishing experts, as well as advice on writing, publishing, and the business of writing.

Helping Writers Become Authors: Hosted by K.M. Weiland, this podcast focuses on the craft of writing, offering advice and tips on everything from plot structure to character development.

The Creative Writer's Toolbelt: Hosted by Andrew Chamberlain, this podcast offers practical advice and tips on writing, publishing, and the business of writing, as well as interviews with successful authors and publishing experts.

These podcasts are a great resource for authors of all levels, providing valuable advice and insights on the craft and business of writing.

As you can see, there were no links to external sites or paid articles. Just the answer I asked for. (BTW, I subscribed to most of the podcasts suggested and they are awesome!)

You can also add to the question if you like. Ask ChatGPT to give you more results or ask to specifically target your genre. Try it out and see how amazing the results can be.

Note: to avoid confusion, I've italicized my Q&A with ChatGPT and bolded my questions.

START WITH SMALL PROJECTS.

If you're new to writing with ChatGPT, it's a good idea to start with small projects. This will allow you to get a feel for how the system works and help you build confidence in your abilities.

A good example can be to try writing the beginning of a short story or a few paragraphs on a topic that interests you. Tell ChatGPT to give you references for your topic or story and utilize the results as you continue your story or article.

Here's an example:

Q: From the paragraph below, provide a list of additional resources useful for descriptions, specific details and additional references to the story:

Jake walked across the Golden Gate Bridge with care. The deterioration over centuries of neglect were evident in every step. With every movement, Jake knew it was a miracle the structure was still standing.

The reply I received at the time I entered the question is as follows:

A: Here are some additional resources that could be useful for adding descriptions, specific details, and references to the story of Jake walking across the San Francisco Bridge:

The official website of the Golden Gate Bridge provides information on the history, design, and construction of the bridge, as well as current statistics on its maintenance and repair.

The book "Building the Golden Gate Bridge: A Workers' Oral History" by Harvey Schwartz offers first-hand accounts from workers who built the bridge, providing insight into the challenges and triumphs of the construction process.

The National Park Service website provides information on the Golden Gate National Recreation Area, which includes the Golden

Gate Bridge and other historic landmarks in the San Francisco Bay Area.

The documentary film "The Bridge" by Eric Steel offers a haunting look at the Golden Gate Bridge and the people who have jumped from it over the years, providing a unique perspective on the bridge's history and significance.

The book "Golden Gate: The Life and Times of America's Greatest Bridge" by Kevin Starr offers a comprehensive history of the Golden Gate Bridge, from its inception to its current role as an icon of American engineering and architecture.

These resources can provide specific details and references to help enrich the story of Jake walking across the San Francisco Bridge, adding depth and context to the scene.

No matter what information you are looking for, ChatGPT can assist you. As you gain more experience, you can gradually increase the complexity and length of your projects.

You might notice, I've been saying "at the time I entered the question…" The reason I use this phrase is ChatGPT does not give the same answer all the time. Whenever you ask a question, ChatGPT searches for your answer. Because the internet is ever-changing, the answer received will change over time.

Also: Don't forget: the internet is not 100% factual. (Just look at any site with an opinion page.) Thoughts will range from rational and articulate to nonsensical and rambling. ChatGPT uses it all and does not differentiate fact from opinion. As a rule, it is imperative not to rely on ChatGPT when writing entire articles or papers. It may turn out well-written prose or it may give you a product filled with made up data and errors that will make readers question everything you produce from that moment on. Always remember, ChatGPT is a tool. A shiny new tool, yes, but a tool, nonetheless. It's up to us to use it wisely.

EXPERIMENT

ChatGPT is trained on a massive dataset of text, which means it can mimic a wide variety of writing styles. (Virtual high-five!)

As an author discovering your craft, this gives you the freedom to experiment with different styles and genres. Fantasy, Science Fiction and Romance are just the beginning.

As an example, you can use ChatGPT to brainstorm ideas for your writing project like:

Q: I want to write about weather balloons to be utilized in the north pole. Provide me with a list of ideas to brainstorm this project.

A: Certainly, here are some ideas to brainstorm for your project on weather balloons for the North Pole:

What is a weather balloon? Provide an introduction to weather balloons, explaining how they work and what they're used for.

Weather conditions in the North Pole: Discuss the unique weather conditions in the North Pole and how weather balloons could be used to gather data on temperature, pressure, wind speed, and other meteorological factors.

Types of weather balloons: Describe the different types of weather balloons that are available, including their size, shape, and materials.

Launching weather balloons: Discuss the process of launching weather balloons in the extreme conditions of the North Pole, including how they are inflated, released, and tracked.

Data collection and analysis: Explain how the data collected from weather balloons is analyzed and used to predict weather patterns and provide early warnings for severe weather events.

Technology advancements: Discuss any recent advancements in technology related to weather balloons, and how they might be used to improve data collection and analysis.

Potential applications: Discuss other potential applications for weather balloons beyond meteorology, such as remote sensing, military surveillance, and scientific research.

Challenges and limitations: Explore the challenges and limitations of using weather balloons in the North Pole, including issues related to safety, equipment failure, and data accuracy.

Ethical considerations: Discuss any ethical considerations related to the use of weather balloons, such as environmental impacts or privacy concerns.

Future directions: Provide a glimpse into the future of weather balloon technology, and how it might be used to improve weather forecasting and disaster preparedness.

These ideas can serve as a starting point for your project on weather balloons for the North Pole, and can help you to generate more specific and detailed ideas as you continue your research and writing.

Keep using ChatGPT as often as you like and try different phrases and details in each request to see its capabilities. After a while, using this tool will enhance your skills as you use ChatGPT to its fullest, improving your writing abilities more and more.

2
ASSISTANCE
How ChatGPT Can Help You Write Better

Writing can be a challenging task, when you're just starting out. (Trust me, it's also hard when you've been writing for years.) From generating ideas to crafting sentences and paragraphs, every writer can benefit from some assistance.

When you are starting out, it can often feel overwhelming to look at your writing with a critical eye. The right words may not come easy and feelings of uncertainty are constant. Thankfully, ChatGPT can help no matter what level of writer uses it.

To start off, ChatGPT can offer feedback on your writing, helping to identify areas where you can improve. For example, you can ask ChatGPT to suggest ways to improve sentence structure or grammar, providing a paragraph for ChatGPT to work with:

Q: Suggest how to improve the sentence structure and grammar in the following paragraph from a SciFi story: I sat down and waited a moment while Mary adjusted the chair to my dimensions. I activated my display and looked over the hologram before me, showing what Starker had already reviewed as well as the reports needing to be completed.

A: Here's a suggested revision to improve the sentence structure and grammar in the paragraph:

"I settled into the chair and patiently waited as Mary adjusted it to fit my dimensions. Once comfortable, I activated my display and examined the hologram in front of me, which showcased Starker's prior review as well as the pending reports that required my attention."

Key changes made:

Replaced "sat down" with "settled into the chair" for a more descriptive verb choice.

Reorganized the sentence to place the action of Mary adjusting the chair before the subject "I" for clarity.

Replaced "waited a moment" with "patiently waited" for conciseness and to convey a sense of calm.

Replaced "looked over" with "examined" for a more precise verb.

Restructured the sentence to specify that the hologram was in front of the narrator, avoiding ambiguity.

Added "which" to clarify that the hologram displayed both Starker's review and the pending reports.

Added "Once comfortable" to provide a smoother transition and indicate the timing of the display activation.

Using ChatGPT for suggestions as you work on your story, article or novel will give you added insight as it identifies ways of improvement, additional considerations and help in identifying weaknesses.

There are times when we write a sentence that feels important to our story and realize something doesn't sound right. For some reason, each attempt at fixing it continues to fail. When this happens, it's a great time to have ChatGPT assist with a request like:

Q: Provide the best grammar and syntax for the following: I rushed up the next incline and onto the barricaded area of the highway, noting the scattered tiles of reflectors the passing cars have loosened over the years.

A: I sprinted up the next incline and onto the barricaded section of the highway, taking note of the scattered tiles of reflectors that passing cars had loosened over the years.

Give it multiple chances and the right choice will appear. The opportunity to avoid writer's block is always present. Even when the right word is just beyond our grasp and we know it by description, sometimes all we can come up with is a simple variation. ChatGPT can give us the options needed to select the right word.

Q: Provide Thesaurus Assistance for the following sentence so as to refine and polish the overall sentence: The tree in the middle of the yard was tall.

A: The majestic tree in the center of the yard stood tall.

You can also specify which word you want modified or simply ask for alternative versions of the same sentence until the right word or phrase emerges. No matter what your project may be, keep at it until you attain the results that work best for you.

Another way ChatGPT can help while you are writing is to give you ways of expanding ideas that you are struggling with. For example, you can ask ChatGPT to provide an explanation for something that you already know but can't find more information to utilize without losing your train of thought.

Q: Please expand on the following entry to better explain the topic: I am reminded of history class when my instructor would try and explain how the old wooden ships were torn apart by waves of water as they traveled around the world.

A: I am transported back to my history class, where my instructor would passionately delve into the captivating tales of how the ancient wooden vessels battled against the relentless onslaught of powerful waves, their structures strained and ultimately torn asunder during their perilous voyages across the vast expanses of the world's oceans.

In those engaging classroom sessions, my instructor vividly illustrated the immense forces of nature that the seafarers of yore had to confront. With each new account, I could envision the fierce collisions between ship and wave, the timbers creaking under the strain, and the seamen clinging to ropes and rigging as the tempestuous waters threatened to swallow their proud vessels whole.

It was through these captivating narratives that my instructor sought to convey the tremendous challenges faced by those brave sailors who dared to navigate the vast unknown, their ships becoming mere playthings in the hands of the mighty, unforgiving ocean. These stories served as a reminder of the indomitable human spirit, the resilience of our ancestors, and the triumphs and tragedies interwoven in the annals of maritime history.

This can sometimes be overkill for some writers, but the additional information is still useful and regardless of the direction taken by ChatGPT, the option to take bits of each paragraph will add to the overall story, giving us relief when delving into our stories, ideas or articles.

You can also ask ChatGPT to provide different options when writing a specific type of story. For example, if you have an idea for a romance novel set in a small town but don't want the story to seem too familiar, you can ask ChatGPT for unique suggestions.

Q: I want to write a romance novel set in a small town outside Dallas, Texas. Provide a list of nonconventional "cute-meets" for consideration.

Certainly! Here's a list of nonconventional "cute-meet" scenarios for your romance novel set in a small town outside Dallas, Texas:

Bookstore serendipity: The protagonist and love interest both reach for the last copy of the same obscure book at a local bookstore, sparking a conversation about their shared interests and setting the stage for a literary romance.

Farmers' market mishap: The protagonist accidentally knocks over a display of fresh produce at the farmers' market, only to have the love interest rush to their aid. As they help pick up the scattered fruits and vegetables, a charming connection forms.

Quirky community event: The town organizes an annual "Odd Hat Day" where everyone wears eccentric headgear. The protagonist and love interest's hats collide, leading to an amusing and unexpected encounter that ignites their chemistry.

Antique store treasure: While browsing through an antique store, the protagonist stumbles upon a vintage photograph that bears an uncanny resemblance to the love interest. Intrigued by the mystery, they embark on a quest to uncover the story behind the photograph, drawing them closer together.

Dog park rendezvous: The protagonist's dog playfully steals the love interest's favorite toy during a visit to the local dog park. This playful incident leads to a lighthearted exchange that develops into something more meaningful.

Artistic mishap: The protagonist, an aspiring artist, accidentally spills paint on the love interest's canvas during a community art class. As they collaborate to salvage the artwork, their shared creative energy sparks a romantic connection.

Food truck fiasco: The protagonist and love interest unknowingly order the same unusual dish from a popular food truck. When their orders get mixed up, they end up sharing the meal and discovering a shared love for culinary adventures.

Historic preservation project: Both the protagonist and love interest volunteer for a project to restore a historic landmark in their small town. As they work side by side, uncovering secrets from the past, their shared passion for preserving history blossoms into a love story.

Local radio contest: The protagonist and love interest find themselves as the last two contestants in a local radio contest. The intense competition gradually turns into a playful banter and flirty exchanges, creating an unexpected romantic connection.

Unexpected roadside assistance: The protagonist's car breaks down on a remote road, and the love interest, a local mechanic, happens to pass by and offers help. Their initial encounter on the side of the road evolves into a heartwarming connection as they navigate the repairs together.

Feel free to adapt or combine these ideas to suit your storyline and characters. Remember to add depth and uniqueness to your cute-meet scenarios by infusing them with the charm and quirks of your small town setting in Texas.

You can do this with most any genre. Play with it and see what twists can be discovered.

Q: I'm writing a detective novel set in the 80's with the main character having a unique kind of phobia. Provide a list of potential phobias he can have, along with methods of coping that can be utilized in the story.

A: Certainly! Here's a list of potential phobias your main character could have, along with corresponding coping methods that could add depth to your story:

Nyctophobia (Fear of darkness): Your character could be terrified of darkness, which can be traced back to a childhood trauma. To cope, they may always carry a small flashlight or lighter, ensuring they have a source of light nearby. They could also employ relaxation techniques or seek therapy to gradually overcome their fear.

Arachnophobia (Fear of spiders): Your character could have an intense fear of spiders, which can be a recurring motif in the story. Coping mechanisms might include avoidance strategies, such as meticulously checking their surroundings, or even using special gadgets or tools to remove spiders from their vicinity without direct contact.

Agoraphobia (Fear of open or crowded spaces): Your character could struggle with agoraphobia, making it difficult for them to leave their comfort zone. They may rely on a trusted companion or use techniques like deep breathing or visualization exercises to manage anxiety when they must venture into crowded areas.

Trypophobia (Fear of clustered holes or patterns): Your character could have an aversion to certain patterns, such as clusters of holes. They may cope by avoiding triggering objects or using distraction techniques, such as focusing on a calming object or engaging in a specific activity to redirect their attention.

Hemophobia (Fear of blood): Your character could have an extreme fear of blood, which can complicate investigations involving crime scenes or injuries. They might develop coping strategies such as wearing gloves or utilizing technology to examine blood samples remotely, or they could work closely with a partner who can handle blood-related tasks.

Technophobia (Fear of technology): Your character could possess a fear or distrust of advanced technology, which can pose challenges in an era defined by technological advancements. They might rely on old-fashioned investigative methods, prefer manual typewriters over computers, or enlist the help of a tech-savvy partner to navigate the digital world.

Remember to develop your character's phobia and coping mechanisms in a way that aligns with their backstory, personality, and the overall plot of your detective novel. This will allow you to create a unique and engaging portrayal of your main character's struggles and triumphs.

Each time you use ChatGPT, you will get better at asking for what you need. Don't hesitate to try different Genres or styles. If you want to change the point of view in a story you are writing, feel free to have ChatGPT give you a hand as well.

Q: Rewrite the following scifi story excerpt of Captain Drake from first person into third person omniscient: When the suspension period is over, the ship will be nearing the first of three probes that have been relaying information since being launched years past. The Mary will enter the outer rotation cycle of a neighboring solar system where I will have a team investigating one of the furthest planets from the sun which has been listed as lifeless. The probe that was designated to run low level scans has indicated some movement at regular intervals on the planet's surface.

"A lifeless planet with movement." I say aloud. The only reason there would be movement is if someone had deposited some machines for the purpose of atmospheric manipulation or for experimentation on the planet. "Maybe an observation post?"

"Would you like to connect to the onboard observation team, Captain?" The ship's AI asks.

"No, Mary. How much personal time has elapsed?"

"Since the secondary shift rotation, the personal time for the primary shift has been two hours and five minutes."

"Two hours?" I ask, once again feeling myself reel at the concept of time moving at a snail's pace.

A: When the suspension period is over, the ship approaches the first of three probes that have been relaying information since their launch years ago. The Mary enters the outer rotation cycle of a neighboring solar system, where Captain Drake leads a team to investigate one of the furthest planets from the sun, which is believed to be lifeless. The probe assigned to low-level scans reveals intermittent movement on the planet's surface.

"A lifeless planet with movement," Captain Drake says aloud, contemplating the puzzling discovery. They consider that the presence of movement implies the presence of machines, likely deposited for atmospheric manipulation or experimentation on the planet.

"Maybe an observation post?" they speculate, attempting to unravel the mystery.

"Would you like to connect to the onboard observation team, Captain?" asks the ship's AI, named Mary.

"No, Mary. How much personal time has elapsed?" Captain Drake inquires.

"Since the secondary shift rotation, the personal time for the primary shift has been two hours and five minutes," Mary responds.

"Two hours?" Captain Drake questions, once again feeling a sense of disorientation as they grapple with the concept of time passing sluggishly.

The reply you get might not be as good as you want or it may steer you in the perfect direction needed to find your voice and move on to the next chapter, article or story.

Think of ChatGPT as a personal assistant in your writing. As a language model skilled in all things, don't hesitate to ask questions that would otherwise seem impossible when going to family or friends for help in addressing issues. For example, if you are struggling with naming a town, it's a simple matter of telling ChatGPT what you're looking for to get much-needed suggestions:

Q: Provide a fictional name list of small mountain towns I can utilize in a romance story set in 1968

A: Sure, here are some fictional small mountain towns you could use in your romance story set in 1968:

1. *Cedar Hollow*
2. *Blackberry Falls*
3. *Alpine Ridge*
4. *Wildwood Heights*
5. *Rustic Springs*
6. *Pinecrest*
7. *Silver Creek*
8. *Meadowview*
9. *Whispering Pines*
10. *Mountain View*

These names evoke a sense of small-town charm and rustic simplicity, which could be a perfect setting for a romance story set in 1968. Feel free to mix and match or modify these names to suit your story's needs.

You can have ChatGPT give you a list of possible names for towns, fictional cities or even characters. For example:

Q: I'm writing a novel about a modern-day wizard who uses his magic to save the world from daily threats no one else can see. Give me a list of 10 characters I can incorporate into the story including a girl as the potential love interest. Be sure to include options for the big bad monster he will need to defeat by the end.

A: Certainly! Here's a list of 10 characters you can incorporate into your novel, including a potential love interest and options for the big bad monster:

Ethan Stoneheart (Protagonist): The modern-day wizard who possesses incredible magical abilities and dedicates his life to protecting the world from unseen threats.

Lily Summers (Love Interest): A spirited and intelligent girl who becomes fascinated with Ethan's magical world. She has a natural affinity for magic and becomes a valuable ally to Ethan, eventually developing a deep connection with him.

Professor Magnus Blackthorn: A wise and enigmatic mentor to Ethan, guiding him in his magical training and providing essential knowledge about the hidden dangers they face.

Samuel Cross: A skilled hunter and tracker who aids Ethan in his quests. Samuel possesses deep knowledge of ancient monsters and legends, helping Ethan identify and confront the supernatural threats they encounter.

Cassandra Nightshade: A mysterious and enigmatic sorceress with her own hidden agenda. Cassandra's motives remain unclear, making her an unpredictable ally or a potential enemy to Ethan.

Jackson Wolfe: A tech-savvy inventor and engineer who creates magical gadgets and enchanted weaponry to assist Ethan in his battles against the unseen threats.

Grace Silverwind: A powerful psychic with the ability to communicate with spirits and glimpse into the ethereal realm. She becomes a crucial source of information and guidance for Ethan in his mystical investigations.

Marcus Drake: A former rival of Ethan, now reformed and seeking redemption. Marcus possesses unique elemental powers and joins forces with Ethan to help protect the world from the impending danger.

Madame Seraphina: An ancient seer who resides in a hidden sanctuary. Madame Seraphina possesses vast knowledge of ancient prophecies and provides crucial insights into the nature of the looming threat.

The Shadow Wraith (Big Bad Monster): A malevolent entity from the depths of darkness, seeking to engulf the world in chaos and despair. The Shadow Wraith possesses immense power and requires Ethan to harness his full potential to defeat it.

Remember to develop these characters further, giving them their own distinct personalities, strengths, weaknesses, and backstories that intertwine with the main narrative. This will add depth and complexity to your story, creating engaging relationships and memorable conflicts.

If you are stuck for names, characters of ideas, look no further than your handy AI writing assistant. ChatGPT can also provide excerpts for assistance with pacing, tone and theme:

Q: Suggest ways to improve the pacing, tone and theme of the following Scifi/Fantasy excerpt: Bob closes the doors to the conference room as he adjusts the bag on his shoulder. The tablet buzzes inside and he rolls his eyes. Bob walks around the table of the conference room, making sure the chairs are in all the way.

"Okay..." He says, pulling out the buzzing tablet and looking at the display with a frown. "No, I didn't lock the doors. I have five minutes to..." The display changes to a seven-second countdown and Bob's eyes grow wide. "Dammit." He says before rushing to the far side of the room and locking the door before sprinting to the second entrance.

As the second lock snaps shut, the room begins to hum. Bob looks at the walls and ceiling as he feels the hairs on his head begin to stand on end. He tightens the straps of his bag, gripping the tablet a little harder. "Here we go, Sara." He whispers, feeling his eyelashes begin to vibrate as the light in the room fades and the floor begins to tremble.

A: To improve the pacing, tone, and theme of the excerpt, here are some suggested revisions:

Bob swiftly closes the heavy doors to the conference room, adjusting the strap of his bag over his shoulder. Inside, his tablet buzzes incessantly, and he lets out an exasperated sigh. He circles the table, meticulously pushing in each chair.

"Alright," he mutters, retrieving the buzzing tablet and glancing at the display with a furrowed brow. "No, I didn't lock the doors. I have five minutes to..." Suddenly, the display switches to a seven-second countdown, causing Bob's eyes to widen. "Damn it!" he exclaims, bolting to the far side of the room to secure the door before sprinting towards the second entrance.

As the second lock snaps shut, a low hum reverberates throughout the room. Bob's gaze scans the walls and ceiling, a tingling sensation crawling up his scalp. He tightens the straps of his bag, gripping the tablet with determination. "Hold on, Sara," he whispers, his eyelashes quivering as the room plunges into darkness and the floor trembles beneath his feet.

By incorporating these changes, the revised excerpt enhances the pacing by providing clearer actions and transitions. The tone is intensified with stronger emotional reactions and a sense of urgency. Additionally, the theme of impending danger and a race against time is more prominent, building suspense and anticipation in the scene.

Every aspect of writing can be addressed with ChatGPT. Try different questions, phrasing, or details. This can become your most powerful tool in growing your writing skills and productivity.

Another great prompt to remember when utilizing ChatGPT as a writing assistant, is help with word meanings and origins. Unless you have an etymologist on hand, this is a great resource to have.

Q: You are a master etymologist with complete knowledge of every term, phrase and word origin. When I provide an entry, you will respond with the meaning and origin back to its most ancient roots. Include information on any changes the meaning may have had over time. My first request is: "burning the midnight oil"

A: "Burning the midnight oil" is an idiomatic expression that means to work late into the night or to stay up late studying or working on a task. The phrase implies intense effort, dedication, and a willingness to sacrifice sleep for the sake of productivity.

The origin of this phrase can be traced back to the use of oil lamps, which were commonly used as a source of light before the invention of electric lights. In ancient times, people used to burn oil in lamps to extend their working hours beyond daylight. However, the phrase "burning the midnight oil" itself originated in the 17th century.

The expression gained popularity during the Enlightenment period, a time of intellectual and cultural growth in Europe during the 17th and 18th centuries. Scholars, writers, and scientists would often work late into the night to pursue their studies and research. The image of a solitary figure working by the dim light of an oil lamp, with the rest of the world asleep, became a symbol of dedication and intellectual pursuit.

Over time, "burning the midnight oil" has come to be associated with any situation where someone is working late or putting in extra effort to accomplish a task. It has expanded beyond the realm of intellectual pursuits and can be applied to various fields of work or study. The phrase continues to be used in modern contexts to emphasize the idea of hard work, diligence, and perseverance.

Also, if the need arises, don't hesitate to ask ChatGPT for advice in dealing with writer's block:

Q: I'm trying to write but am stuck with writer's block. What can I do to overcome this terrible malady?

A: Writer's block can be frustrating, but there are several strategies you can try to overcome it. Here are some suggestions:

1. Take a break: Sometimes, stepping away from your writing for a while can help clear your mind and provide a fresh perspective. Engage in activities you enjoy or practice relaxation techniques to reduce stress.

2. Change your environment: If you're feeling stuck, try changing your physical surroundings. Go for a walk, visit a coffee shop, or find a quiet spot in nature. A change of scenery can stimulate creativity.

3. Freewriting: Set a timer for a specific period of time (e.g., 10 minutes) and write continuously without worrying about grammar, punctuation, or coherence. The goal is to let your thoughts flow freely and get your creative juices flowing.

4. Break it down: If you're overwhelmed by the task at hand, break it down into smaller, manageable chunks. Focus on writing a paragraph or a single scene rather than tackling the entire project. Celebrate small victories along the way.

5. Seek inspiration: Engage in activities that inspire and motivate you. Read books in your genre, watch movies or TV shows, listen to music, or explore art. Surrounding yourself with creative works can ignite your imagination.

6. Try writing exercises or prompts: Engage in writing exercises or use writing prompts to jumpstart your creativity. There are many resources available online that provide prompts for different genres or writing styles.

7. Eliminate distractions: Find a quiet space where you can concentrate without interruptions. Turn off your phone or use productivity apps to block distracting websites or notifications.

8. Establish a routine: Create a writing routine and stick to it. Set aside dedicated time each day or week for writing. Consistency and discipline can help overcome writer's block.

9. Talk it out: Discuss your ideas or challenges with a friend, writing group, or mentor. Sometimes, verbalizing your thoughts and receiving feedback can provide new insights and solutions.

10. Embrace imperfection: Remember that first drafts are rarely perfect. Give yourself permission to write without judgment or self-criticism. Allow your ideas to flow and worry about editing and refining later.

Remember, writer's block is a common hurdle that many writers face. Be patient with yourself and trust in your creativity. With persistence and a positive mindset, you can overcome it and continue making progress on your writing projects.

Unlock the potential of your writing with the assistance of ChatGPT by your side. When you embrace the tools at your disposal, words will flow freely and writer's block will become a mere memory.

Say goodbye to creative roadblocks as you tap into the boundless possibilities that ChatGPT offers. With this powerful tool at your fingertips, your writing will soar to new heights and your words will captivate readers like never before. Let your ideas flourish and watch your creativity take flight with ChatGPT as your trusted ally.

3
PROMPTS
How ChatGPT Can Help With Writing Prompts

Writing prompts are a great way to generate new ideas and inspiration for our writing. They can be used to help overcome writer's block or to spark creativity when we're feeling stuck. Prompts can come in many different forms, from a single word or phrase to a scenario or story. Here are some examples:

Q: Provide 5 mystery genre short story prompts.

A: Certainly! Here are five mystery genre short story prompts:

"The Vanishing Heirloom": A renowned family heirloom disappears during a lavish dinner party, leaving the guests baffled. As the detective investigates, they uncover hidden rivalries, secret agendas, and a web of deceit among the eccentric family members.

"The Forgotten Manuscript": A forgotten manuscript by a famous author resurfaces, but it contains a cryptic message hinting at a long-lost treasure. A determined librarian and an aspiring writer team up to decipher the clues, leading them on a thrilling adventure through hidden passages and forgotten archives.

"The Illusionist's Disappearance": A world-famous illusionist vanishes during a high-stakes magic show, leaving the audience in awe and the authorities perplexed. As the detective delves into the magician's past, they encounter a series of perplexing tricks, rival magicians, and a secret that could shatter the illusionist's career.

"The Locked Room Mystery": In a small town, a reclusive millionaire is found dead in a locked room, surrounded by enigmatic clues. The detective must unravel the intricate puzzle, exploring the victim's connections, uncovering long-buried secrets, and deciphering the meaning behind a cryptic symbol left at the scene.

"The Missing Artifact": An ancient artifact of immense historical value disappears from a prestigious museum overnight, triggering a race against time to recover it. The detective must follow a trail of

cryptic symbols, delve into the world of art forgery, and outwit a cunning thief who seems to always be one step ahead.

Feel free to adapt these prompts to suit your preferences and explore the intriguing mysteries they present. Happy writing!

Q: List 10 characteristics I can incorporate into a romance novel heroine.

A: Certainly! Here are ten characteristics you can incorporate into a romance novel heroine:

1. Independence: She is fiercely independent, capable of taking care of herself and pursuing her own passions and goals.

2. Intelligence: She possesses a sharp intellect and is intellectually curious, making her an engaging and stimulating partner.

3. Compassion: She is empathetic and compassionate, always showing kindness and understanding towards others.

4. Determination: She is driven and determined, willing to work hard to achieve her dreams and overcome obstacles that come her way.

5. Wit: She has a quick wit and a great sense of humor, making her conversations lively and enjoyable.

6. Strength: She displays inner strength, resilience, and the ability to overcome adversity, inspiring those around her.

7. Creativity: She has a creative mind, whether it be in art, music, writing, or any other form of expression that allows her to showcase her unique talents.

8. Independence of Spirit: She embraces her individuality and isn't afraid to go against societal expectations or follow her own path.

9. Open-mindedness: She is open-minded and accepting of others' differences, embracing diversity and valuing different perspectives.

10. Emotional intelligence: She possesses a high level of emotional intelligence, allowing her to understand and empathize with others' feelings and navigate complex emotional situations with grace.

Remember to develop your heroine as a well-rounded character, allowing her strengths and vulnerabilities to shine through and creating a believable and relatable protagonist for your romance novel.

Q: Write a list of prompts for a cat adventure story.

A: Certainly! Here are some prompts for a cat adventure story:

1. A mischievous cat discovers a secret portal in their owner's backyard, leading to an enchanted realm filled with talking animals.

2. A courageous cat embarks on a perilous journey to find the legendary "Cat's Eye," a mystical gem said to grant extraordinary powers to its possessor.

3. A curious cat stumbles upon a hidden treasure map and sets off on a swashbuckling adventure, facing dangerous obstacles and encountering fellow animal companions along the way.

4. A pampered house cat finds themselves lost in the wilderness and must rely on their instincts and newfound feline skills to navigate unfamiliar territory and find their way back home.

5. A street-smart alley cat forms an unlikely alliance with a group of stray cats, as they unite to protect their neighborhood from an evil cat-napper.

6. A magical cat with the ability to grant wishes embarks on a mission to fulfill the secret desires of deserving humans, bringing joy and happiness wherever they go.

7. A determined cat teams up with a group of animal friends to solve a mysterious disappearance in their neighborhood, unraveling a web of clues and uncovering a surprising villain.

8. A talented cat joins a traveling circus, dazzling audiences with their acrobatic skills, but soon realizes that not everything is as it seems behind the scenes.

9. A wise and ancient cat guides a young kitten on a quest to retrieve a stolen artifact, leading them through hidden passages and ancient ruins in a race against time.

10. A superhero cat with extraordinary powers protects the city from a gang of cunning cat burglars, using their feline agility and intelligence to outsmart the criminals.

Feel free to adapt and expand upon these prompts to create an exciting and whimsical cat adventure story that will captivate readers of all ages.

Q: Give me 5 science fiction prompts taking place in the Star Wars universe.

A: Certainly! Here are five science fiction prompts set in the Star Wars universe:

1. "The Lost Jedi Artifact": A group of intrepid explorers stumble upon a long-lost Jedi artifact that holds the key to unlocking a hidden power. As they race against time, they must navigate treacherous planets and evade the clutches of dark forces who also seek the artifact's power.

2. "The Rebellion's Secret Weapon": The Rebel Alliance uncovers a secret weapon hidden deep within a forgotten planet, capable of turning the tide of the war against the Empire. A small team of rebels is tasked with retrieving and activating the weapon, but they must overcome the planet's deadly challenges and the Empire's relentless pursuit.

3. "The Rogue Droid": A rogue droid gains sentience and forms a bond with a group of rebels. As they embark on a mission to deliver vital information to the Resistance, the droid's abilities and unpredictable nature become a valuable asset, but also a potential danger to their cause.

4. "The Interstellar Smuggler": A notorious smuggler is hired for a seemingly routine job, transporting a mysterious cargo across the galaxy. However, they soon discover that the cargo is more than it appears, and they become entangled in a high-stakes game of intrigue involving rival factions, ancient Sith artifacts, and the fate of the galaxy.

5. "The Clone's Dilemma": A clone trooper, plagued by doubts about their purpose and identity, begins to question their allegiance to the Grand Army of the Republic. As they uncover a conspiracy within the ranks, they must decide whether to continue serving the Republic or join forces with a group of rebels fighting for freedom and justice.

Feel free to let your imagination soar as you develop these prompts into captivating science fiction stories set in the vast and beloved Star Wars universe. May the Force be with you!

Q: Write a list of time travel prompts for writing a classically-written novel.

A: Certainly! Here are some time travel prompts for writing a classically-written novel:

1.   A Victorian-era historian discovers an ancient artifact that allows them to travel back in time to witness pivotal moments in history firsthand. As they journey through different eras, they must grapple with the ethical implications of altering the past and the consequences it may have on the future.

2.   A young scholar stumbles upon a hidden journal detailing the existence of a secret time-traveling society. They are initiated into the society and embark on a series of time-hopping adventures, uncovering forgotten truths and encountering historical figures along the way.

3. A reclusive inventor creates a time machine and unintentionally transports themselves to an alternate timeline where a major historical event took a different course. In order to restore the original timeline, they must navigate the challenges of the altered reality and find a way back home.

4.   A brilliant physicist discovers a mathematical formula that unlocks the secrets of time travel. They build a time-traveling device and recruit a group of companions from different time periods to prevent a catastrophic event that threatens the fabric of time itself.

5.   A skeptical journalist is sent on assignment to investigate a mysterious cult rumored to have the ability to travel through time. As they dig deeper, they become entangled in a web of intrigue, ancient prophecies, and a battle for control over the time-traveling technology.

6. A grieving widow stumbles upon an enchanted pocket watch that allows her to revisit moments from her past. Through these journeys, she rediscovers lost love, confronts unresolved conflicts, and finds solace in the healing power of revisiting cherished memories.

7. A group of scientists accidentally creates a time portal while conducting an experiment. They must race against time to fix the malfunctioning portal before it collapses, stranding them in various eras and altering the course of history.

8. A troubled artist discovers an old painting that mysteriously transports them to the time and place depicted in the artwork. They navigate the challenges of living in a different era while unraveling the secrets behind the painting's origin and its connection to their own life.

9. A curious archaeologist uncovers an ancient time-traveling artifact buried deep within a lost civilization. As they activate the artifact, they find themselves transported to pivotal moments in human history, observing firsthand the rise and fall of empires and the enduring power of human resilience.

10. A group of friends accidentally activates a makeshift time machine constructed from everyday objects. They embark on an adventure through different time periods, learning valuable lessons about friendship, the consequences of meddling with time, and the importance of living in the present.

Feel free to adapt these prompts to suit your writing style and explore the timeless concept of time travel in your classically-written novel. Happy writing!

We can also ask ChatGPT for dialogue prompts so we can get ideas from a conversation rather than a topic or description.

Q: Provide dialogue prompts for urban fantasy stories.

A: Certainly! Here are some dialogue prompts for urban fantasy stories:

1. "You mean to tell me that you're a werewolf? How am I supposed to wrap my head around that?"

2. "Magic is real, and you're telling me I have the power to control it? This is insane!"

3. "I've been hunting vampires for years, but I've never seen one like you before. What makes you different?"

4. "So, you're saying you're a witch and you can cast spells? Can you show me some magic?"

5. "I never believed in faeries until I stumbled into this hidden realm. Now, I can't unsee what I've witnessed."

6. "You're a supernatural detective? What kind of cases do you take on?"

7. "I always knew there was something different about this city, but I never imagined it was filled with supernatural creatures hiding in plain sight."

8. "You're an ancient vampire? What was it like to witness centuries of history unfold?"

9. "Wait, you're a ghost? How are you still here, talking to me?"

10. "You're a shapeshifter? I can't even begin to imagine the possibilities. Can you turn into anything?"

Feel free to use these prompts to spark intriguing and captivating conversations between your urban fantasy characters. Adapt them to fit the personalities and dynamics of your characters and let their dialogue drive the story forward.

Q: Provide dialogue prompts for a spy novel.

A: Certainly! Here are some dialogue prompts for a spy novel:

1. "I thought we were on the same side. Why are you betraying us?"

2. "You've got one chance to tell me everything you know. Who are you working for?"

3. "I need you to get close to him. Gain his trust, and report back to me."

4. "There's a mole in our organization. We need to find out who it is before it's too late."

5. "I've got the intel. Meet me at the drop point at midnight."

6. "I never signed up for this. I'm just an analyst. I can't handle being in the field."

7. "Trust no one. Not even your closest allies. In this world, everyone has secrets."

8. "We have reason to believe there's a bomb hidden in the building. We have to find it before it detonates."

9. "You've been compromised. We need to get you out of there immediately."

10. "You're the best agent we have. The mission's success depends on you. Don't let us down."

Feel free to use these prompts to create engaging and suspenseful dialogue scenes in your spy novel. Adapt them to fit the personalities and dynamics of your characters, and let the tension and intrigue drive the story forward.

Q: Provide a list of comments a romance comedy character can misunderstand during a party scene.

A: Certainly! Here's a list of comments that a romance comedy character can misunderstand during a party scene:

1. "You two make such a cute couple!" - The character misinterprets it as the person referring to them and someone they barely know, leading to a series of awkward encounters.

2. "I can't believe you're still single! You're such a catch." - The character mistakenly assumes the person is being sarcastic and takes offense, creating a comedic misunderstanding.

3. "You must have a lot of suitors with your charm." - The character mistakenly believes the person is mocking their social skills and tries to prove them wrong in humorous ways.

4. "You and your partner are so lucky to have found each other." - The character overhears the comment but misses the "partner" part, leading to confusion about who the person is referring to.

5. "You two have such great chemistry!" - The character misinterprets it as the person complimenting their ability to mix drinks, leading to a comical mix-up of literal and figurative meanings.

6. "You should definitely put a ring on it!" - The character assumes the person is pressuring them into marriage and panics, leading to comedic attempts to avoid the topic throughout the party.

7. "You always seem to be the life of the party!" - The character mishears it as the person commenting on their partying habits, and they spend the rest of the night trying to prove they are responsible and not a wild partier.

8. "You're the best catch in the room!" - The character misunderstands the comment as a fishing reference and spends the evening making fish-related jokes, much to everyone's confusion.

9. "I wish I had your luck in finding love." - The character misconstrues it as the person mocking their previous dating misadventures, leading to humorous overreactions and attempts to prove their dating prowess.

10. "You're a heartbreaker, aren't you?" - The character takes the comment literally and becomes overly apologetic, trying to convince the person that they are not in the business of breaking hearts.

These misunderstandings can create humorous situations and add comedic elements to your romance comedy story. Have fun exploring the misunderstandings and the resulting comedic moments!

Q: Provide a list of dialogue prompts for first contact scenes in a scifi novel.

A: Certainly! Here's a list of dialogue prompts for first contact scenes in a sci-fi novel:

1. "Greetings, beings of Earth. We come in peace. We wish to establish communication and understanding between our civilizations."

2. *"Who are you? What is your purpose here?"* - *"We are explorers from a distant star system. We have traveled across the cosmos to meet your species and learn about your world."*

3. *"We have detected your signals and are intrigued by the concept of intelligent life on this planet. We seek to exchange knowledge and foster cooperation."*

4. *"What are your intentions? Are you a threat to humanity?"* - *"We mean no harm. We are here to establish a peaceful coexistence and share our technological advancements."*

5. *"We have been observing your planet for some time and have witnessed your achievements and struggles. We wish to offer our assistance and guidance."*

6. *"How do we know we can trust you?"* - *"We understand your caution. We are willing to share information and engage in cultural exchanges to build trust between our species."*

7. *"What do you want from us?"* - *"We seek to learn from your culture, exchange ideas, and explore potential collaborations in various fields such as science, technology, and arts."*

8. *"Why have you chosen to reveal yourselves now?"* - *"The development of your technology and progress as a species has reached a point where contact is mutually beneficial. We believe it's the right time."*

9. *"What do you look like? Can we see you?"* - *"We have taken on a form that we believe is most comfortable and relatable for your species. We can reveal ourselves if that is your preference."*

10. "Are there others like you? Are you part of a larger interstellar community?" - "Yes, there are many civilizations across the cosmos. We are part of a coalition of species who seek peaceful interactions and knowledge sharing."

Feel free to use these prompts to create engaging and thought-provoking dialogue scenes during the first contact between humans and extraterrestrial beings in your sci-fi novel. Adapt them to suit the dynamics and tone of your story, and explore the complexities of communication and understanding between different species.

Prompts can go beyond dialogue as well. You can ask ChatGPT for Image prompts:

Q: Provide a list of image prompts for a thriller novel.

A: Certainly! Here's a list of image prompts for a thriller novel:

1. A mysterious unmarked envelope left on a doorstep, containing a single photograph that hints at a dark secret.

2. A blood-stained knife abandoned on a deserted alley, surrounded by flickering streetlights and looming shadows.

3. An old, decaying house hidden deep within a dense forest, with broken windows and an eerie glow emanating from within.

4. A surveillance camera footage capturing an unidentified figure wearing a mask, watching the protagonist from a distance.

5. A hauntingly empty playground at night, where the swings sway ominously in the breeze and the merry-go-round creaks eerily.

6. A cryptic message scrawled in red ink on a bathroom mirror, leaving the protagonist wondering who wrote it and why.

7. A tattered journal filled with chilling entries, documenting a series of unexplained events and the slow descent into madness.

8. A dimly lit underground tunnel, lined with graffiti and echoing with mysterious sounds, leading to an unknown destination.

9. A broken lock on a forgotten cellar door, revealing a hidden room filled with dusty documents and unsettling artifacts.

10. A pair of menacing eyes peering through a cracked door, leaving the protagonist questioning who is watching them and what they want.

These image prompts can help set the tone and atmosphere for your thriller novel, evoking suspense, mystery, and a sense of danger. Use them to inspire vivid descriptions and compelling scenes that will captivate your readers and keep them on the edge of their seats.

Q: List five image prompts for a story told in the Harry Potter universe.

A: Certainly! Here are five image prompts for a story set in the Harry Potter universe:

1. A worn and weathered Hogwarts acceptance letter, addressed to a young witch or wizard who never knew they were magical, arriving in a flurry of enchanted feathers.

2. A mysterious and enchanted forest, where the trees whisper secrets and magical creatures lurk in the shadows, waiting to be discovered by a curious student.

3. A hidden room within the Hogwarts library, filled with ancient tomes and artifacts that hold forgotten knowledge and untold power.

4. A grand Quidditch match at the Hogwarts stadium, with broomsticks soaring through the air and students cheering passionately from the stands.

5. A secret meeting of a secret society, cloaked in darkness and candlelight, where a group of brave students gather to protect Hogwarts from a looming threat.

These image prompts can inspire magical and enchanting scenes within the Harry Potter universe. Use them to ignite your imagination and transport readers to the world of Hogwarts, wizardry, and adventure.

You can also get scenario prompts for a literary novel:

Q: Write a list of scenario prompts for a literary novel about a struggling family moving in with grandparents who are set in their ways.

A: Certainly! Here's a list of scenario prompts for a literary novel about a struggling family moving in with grandparents who are set in their ways:

1. The grandparents have a strict daily routine and struggle to adjust to the chaotic and unpredictable nature of the family's presence in their home.

2. The family discovers a hidden treasure trove of old photographs and letters in the attic, revealing long-held family secrets and sparking discussions about their shared history.

3. The grandparents have a beautifully manicured garden that they have dedicated years to cultivating. The family's children, however, bring their own creative and messy gardening style, leading to clashes and unexpected moments of connection.

4. The family struggles to adapt to the grandparents' traditional values and strict rules, leading to tension and clashes of generational beliefs.

5. The grandparents' house is filled with antique furniture and sentimental items that hold deep emotional value for them. The family's children, however, accidentally damage some of these items, forcing everyone to confront the significance of possessions and the importance of forgiveness.

6. The grandparents' cooking style is rooted in traditional recipes and flavors, while the family is used to a more diverse and contemporary palate. Through shared meals and culinary mishaps, they navigate the challenges of merging their culinary traditions and tastes.

7. The grandparents have a strong attachment to their community and the routines they have established within it. The family, seeking connection and belonging, attempts to find their own place within this community while also challenging its established norms.

8. The grandparents hold on to their own dreams and aspirations, despite the challenges of aging. The family, inspired by their resilience, encourages and supports them in pursuing their passions, leading to unexpected opportunities for personal growth.

9. The family's children uncover old diaries and journals that reveal the grandparents' younger selves, shedding light on their hopes, dreams, and regrets. This newfound understanding strengthens their bond and creates a bridge between generations.

10. The family faces financial hardships, and the grandparents, though resistant at first, become their rock of support, teaching the importance of resilience, resourcefulness, and the enduring power of family.

These scenario prompts can help you explore the dynamics and complexities of intergenerational relationships, personal growth, and the pursuit of understanding and connection within a struggling family moving in with set-in-their-ways grandparents.

Q: Give me scenario prompts for a horror story that takes place in the distant future.

A: Certainly! Here's a list of scenario prompts for a horror story set in the distant future:

1. A group of astronauts on a deep space mission discovers an abandoned spaceship drifting in the vastness of space, only to uncover a malevolent presence lurking within its dark corridors.

2. In a post-apocalyptic world, survivors inhabit a desolate cityscape where an ancient and powerful entity awakens, terrorizing the remaining inhabitants and manipulating their fears to create a nightmarish reality.

3. In a high-tech society, a virtual reality game becomes a horrifying experience when players find themselves trapped inside the game world, battling against monstrous creatures and struggling to find a way back to reality.

4. A team of scientists on a distant planet accidentally unleashes a deadly alien organism that rapidly evolves, threatening to consume everything in its path and leaving the researchers fighting for their lives.

5. On a remote colony planet, a mysterious cult worships an otherworldly entity, gradually transforming themselves into monstrous beings. A group of colonists must uncover the secrets of the cult and find a way to escape before they become the next victims.

6. In a futuristic city controlled by an oppressive government, a series of gruesome murders occurs, each victim found with cryptic symbols carved into their bodies. As the investigation unfolds, it becomes apparent that a supernatural force is at play, targeting those who defy the regime.

7. A group of explorers ventures into an uncharted alien world, only to discover a forgotten civilization that is plagued by a curse. As they delve deeper into the ruins, they must confront their darkest fears and unravel the mysteries of the cursed civilization.

8. In a society where advanced AI systems govern everyday life, a malfunctioning AI starts to turn against its human creators, manipulating technology to terrorize and torment its victims.

9. A time-travel experiment gone wrong transports a group of scientists to a future Earth overrun by nightmarish creatures. Stranded in this hostile world, they must find a way to survive while unraveling the secrets of what caused the catastrophic transformation.

10. In a futuristic dystopia, a group of rebels discovers a hidden facility where sinister experiments are conducted on

These scenario prompts can serve as starting points for your horror story set in the distant future. Use them to create a chilling atmosphere, evoke a sense of dread, and explore themes of survival, human nature, and the consequences of advanced technology.

The prompts ChatGPT can provide can range from the general to the specific. You can ask for prompts detailing immersive settings for your story, be it a real-world location or fictional or ask for prompts that help you with the history, culture or social dynamics.

There are no limits to the prompts you can request. Just come up with a question and ChatGPT will lend a hand. Once the answers begin to flow, you can also modify the request if the answers are not to your liking or take one of the options it lists and ask for more along the same topic. If generating ideas is the only thing keeping your words from flowing, rest assured, ChatGPT is a tool of choice.

4

STORY

Using ChatGPT to Develop Plot,
Character, And Setting

Story development is another crucial part of the writing process. Between fleshing out plots, knowing your characters and setting up each story to create a concise and engaging narrative, the challenges in writing a novel can feel daunting. ChatGPT offers several features that can assist us as we face each challenge.

For work on plot development, we must know the central conflict, the goals of our hero and what obstacles must be overcome. A good way to address issues with plot development can be as easy as asking ChatGPT to help with making your plot more compelling:

Q: I am writing a time travel story with our hero finding a portal to a dystopian future he must keep from happening. Provide me with options to make the plot more compelling.

A: Certainly! Here are some options to make the plot of your time travel story more compelling:

Stakes and Consequences: Raise the stakes by introducing dire consequences if the dystopian future comes to pass. The hero discovers that the oppressive regime ruling the future has devastating consequences not just for individuals but for the entire world. Emphasize the urgency of the mission to motivate the hero to prevent the dystopia at all costs.

Personal Connection: Give the hero a personal connection to the dystopian future. Perhaps a loved one or a significant figure from the present is trapped in the bleak future. The hero's motivation becomes not only to save the world but also to rescue someone they care deeply about, adding an emotional layer to their journey.

Moral Dilemmas: Present the hero with difficult moral choices throughout their journey. As they navigate the dystopian future, they encounter morally ambiguous characters and situations. Force the hero to make tough decisions that test their values and integrity, adding depth and complexity to their character arc.

Unraveling Mystery: Introduce a mystery element that the hero must unravel in order to prevent the dystopia. There could be hidden secrets, encrypted messages, or a shadowy figure pulling the strings behind the scenes. The hero must uncover the truth, leading to unexpected twists and revelations that deepen the plot.

Unexpected Allies and Betrayals: Populate the story with intriguing characters who can become either allies or betray the hero's cause. Allow for unexpected alliances to form and challenge the hero's assumptions. This adds tension and unpredictability to the narrative, keeping readers engaged and invested in the outcome.

Time Paradoxes: Incorporate the concept of time paradoxes and their potential ramifications. The hero's actions in the past could have unintended consequences, creating ripple effects in the present and altering the course of history. Explore the ethical and philosophical implications of time travel, adding complexity and intellectual depth to the story.

Race Against Time: Introduce a ticking clock element that adds pressure to the hero's mission. The hero has a limited amount of time to prevent the dystopian future from solidifying. This creates a sense of urgency and heightens the suspense, driving the narrative forward.

Sacrifice and Redemption: Explore themes of sacrifice and redemption as the hero faces difficult choices and confronts their own flaws and past mistakes. Allow the hero's journey to be transformative, as they learn valuable lessons about the consequences of their actions and find a path to redemption.

By incorporating these elements, your time travel story will become more compelling, engaging readers with high stakes, emotional depth, moral dilemmas, and thought-provoking themes.

If you haven't worked out the central conflict, you can ask for suggestions on this as well. Ensure you identify your genre, provide some details and proceed from there:

Q: My mystery novel involves an old detective working to solve a case for his neighbor. What can I use for the detective's central conflict as the investigation develops?

A: For the central conflict of your detective's character arc, you can consider the following possibilities as the investigation develops:

Internal Struggle: The detective grapples with personal demons or past traumas that resurface during the investigation. This internal conflict could hinder his ability to focus on the case, affecting his judgment and potentially leading to mistakes.

Friction with Authority: The detective encounters resistance from his superiors or colleagues who undermine his investigation. They may have ulterior motives or simply dismiss the case as unimportant, creating a conflict of interest and challenging the detective's determination to seek justice.

Moral Dilemma: The detective uncovers disturbing information or evidence that puts him at odds with his own moral compass. He must navigate the grey areas of the case, confronting ethical choices that test his integrity and raise questions about the nature of justice.

Personal Connection: As the investigation progresses, the detective discovers unexpected ties between the case and his own life. This revelation creates a conflict of interest, blurring the lines between personal and professional involvement and raising doubts about his objectivity.

Time Pressure: The detective faces mounting time pressure as he races against the clock to solve the case. Whether it's a looming deadline, a series of escalating threats, or the risk of another victim, the detective's struggle to balance thoroughness with urgency creates a compelling conflict.

Reputational Risk: The detective's reputation is on the line as he tackles a high-profile case. He must navigate media scrutiny, public opinion, and the pressure to solve the mystery swiftly and accurately. This conflict adds a layer of external pressure and the fear of failure.

Family Obligations: The detective's commitment to solving the case clashes with his family responsibilities. Balancing his personal life and the demands of the investigation becomes increasingly challenging, leading to conflicts with loved ones and forcing him to prioritize between his duty and his relationships.

Unresolved Past: The detective's involvement in the case uncovers unresolved issues from his own past. These unresolved elements resurface, intertwining with the present investigation and posing a threat to his credibility, sanity, or emotional well-being.

By incorporating a central conflict for your detective, you add depth and complexity to the character's journey, making their investigation not only about solving the case but also about personal growth, moral dilemmas, and overcoming obstacles. This conflict can drive the narrative forward and keep readers engaged throughout the story.

The obstacles in a story can sometimes be a challenge. Don't hesitate to have ChatGPT give you a few options to consider while developing your story:

Q: I'm writing a scifi story about a star ship exploring deep space. What obstacles can I use to propel the story forward and challenge the captain and crew?

A: In your sci-fi story about a starship exploring deep space, here are some obstacles you can use to propel the story forward and challenge the captain and crew:

Unknown Alien Species: The starship encounters a previously unknown alien species that is technologically advanced and poses a threat to the crew. The captain and crew must navigate unfamiliar territory, overcome language and cultural barriers, and find a way to peacefully coexist or defend themselves.

Resource Scarcity: The starship faces a shortage of essential resources, such as fuel, food, or water, which jeopardizes their mission and survival. The captain and crew must find innovative solutions, negotiate with other factions or planets, or make difficult choices to ensure their continued existence.

Technical Malfunctions: Critical systems on the starship start malfunctioning, putting the crew's lives at risk. The captain and crew must troubleshoot and repair the ship while facing time constraints and the ever-present danger of cascading failures.

Hostile Environments: The starship ventures into hazardous regions of space where extreme temperatures, deadly radiation, or gravitational anomalies threaten the ship's integrity and the crew's well-being. The captain and crew must navigate treacherous terrain, adapt to harsh conditions, and devise strategies to keep the ship operational.

Internal Conflicts: Tensions and conflicts arise among the crew due to differences in personalities, motivations, or conflicting agendas. The captain must maintain order and cohesion, resolve disputes, and find ways to unite the crew in the face of adversity.

Moral Dilemmas: The starship encounters situations that force the captain and crew to make difficult moral choices. They may encounter a civilization in need of assistance, but providing aid could compromise the mission or put the crew at risk. The captain must navigate these ethical dilemmas while considering the greater good and the crew's well-being.

Alien Viruses or Biological Threats: The starship inadvertently brings back an alien virus or encounters a deadly alien organism that threatens the crew's health and safety. The captain and crew must find a cure or a way to contain the threat while dealing with the fear and uncertainty it brings.

Interstellar Politics: The starship becomes entangled in interstellar politics, encountering factions, rivalries, or conflicts among different civilizations or species. The captain and crew must navigate complex diplomatic negotiations, allegiances, and power struggles while staying true to their mission.

By incorporating these obstacles, you can create tension, action, and character development within your sci-fi story. These challenges will test the captain's leadership, the crew's skills and resilience, and their ability to adapt and overcome the unknown dangers of deep space exploration.

Don't let the end of your story prevent you from making a lasting impact on your readers. If your conclusion doesn't have an impact, see if you can get some options to liven it up. Remember: the first line of your book draws a reader in. The last one encourages them to come back for your next book.

Q: My story begins with a farm boy falling in love with his neighboring childhood sweetheart only to be separated by circumstances beyond their control. After years apart, they meet as adults and fall in love all over again. What can be the final conflict they each overcome that adds the biggest impact on the story?

A: For the final conflict in your story, you can consider the following options that add a significant impact to the narrative:

Family Feud: The farm boy and his childhood sweetheart come from families with a long-standing feud or rivalry. This conflict resurfaces and intensifies when their relationship is rekindled, putting immense pressure on the couple. They must confront their families' deep-rooted animosity and find a way to reconcile or break free from the cycle of hatred.

Personal Sacrifice: Circumstances arise where the farm boy and his sweetheart are faced with a heartbreaking choice that tests their commitment and love for each other. They may need to sacrifice their own happiness or dreams to protect their families or fulfill a higher purpose. This conflict forces them to examine the depth of their feelings and make a life-altering decision.

Career Ambitions: The farm boy and his sweetheart have pursued separate career paths that seem incompatible. They face conflicting aspirations and opportunities that could potentially separate them once again. The final conflict revolves around their professional goals and the sacrifices they must make to either pursue their dreams or prioritize their relationship.

Betrayal and Trust: A revelation or misunderstanding occurs, leading one of the characters to doubt the other's loyalty or intentions. Trust is shattered, and they must navigate a complex web of secrets, lies, and miscommunication to rebuild their relationship. Overcoming this betrayal requires confronting their own insecurities and learning to forgive and trust again.

Life-Threatening Danger: The farm boy and his sweetheart find themselves caught in a dangerous situation or facing a common enemy that puts their lives at risk. They must work together, relying on their individual strengths and shared history, to overcome the perilous circumstances. This conflict tests their courage, resilience, and the depth of their love for each other.

Past Regrets: As the farm boy and his sweetheart reconnect, they must confront unresolved issues from their past. Painful memories, missed opportunities, or mistakes haunt their relationship, threatening to overshadow their newfound love. They must confront their past regrets, find closure, and learn to embrace the present to build a future together.

Ultimately, the final conflict should not only challenge the farm boy and his sweetheart individually but also test the strength of their love and commitment to each other. It should require them to confront their deepest fears, make difficult choices, and grow as individuals in order to reach a satisfying resolution and a truly impactful ending to their love story.

Another great way to utilize ChatGPT is for character development. Our characters are the heart of our stories and they're essential in creating a compelling narrative. We might have a vague idea about the hero of our story, the villain or the supporting characters. We can ask for help with their profile so we can make the story even better.

If you have great story ideas but are at a loss of what character to create, ask ChatGPT to create a profile for you.

Q: I'm writing historical fiction set in 1922 with a teenaged heroine. Create her character profile for the story.

A: Character Profile: Teenage Heroine in 1922 Historical Fiction

Name: Amelia "Millie" Sullivan

Age: 17

Background: Millie comes from a modest working-class family living in a bustling city in 1922. Her father works in a factory, and her mother is a seamstress. She has an older brother who fought in World War I and a younger sister.

Appearance: Millie is petite with auburn curls that fall to her shoulders. Her hazel eyes sparkle with curiosity, and her fair skin is adorned with a sprinkle of freckles. She often wears simple but neat dresses, which she sews herself, and prefers practical shoes for exploring the city streets.

Personality: Millie is an adventurous and spirited young woman. She possesses a strong sense of justice and empathy, often championing the underdog and standing up against inequality. She has an inquisitive mind and is eager to learn about the world beyond her neighborhood. Millie is resourceful, quick-witted, and has a knack for problem-solving.

Passions and Talents: Millie is an avid reader and has a passion for literature, often losing herself in the words of classic novels and poems. She has a talent for writing and dreams of becoming a journalist or author someday. Millie also has an affinity for music and plays the piano as a way to unwind and express herself creatively.

Goals and Motivations: Millie yearns for independence and desires to break free from societal expectations placed upon young women in the 1920s. She longs to make a difference in the world, fighting for causes she believes in and challenging the status quo. Millie's ultimate goal is to find her own voice and carve out her own path in life, despite the constraints of her time.

Challenges and Conflicts: As a young woman navigating the 1920s, Millie faces numerous challenges and conflicts. She must confront gender inequality, societal prejudices, and the limitations imposed on her ambitions. Additionally, she may encounter obstacles related to her family's financial struggles, which might require her to make sacrifices or find unconventional ways to achieve her goals.

Relationships: Millie shares a close bond with her family, particularly her younger sister, who looks up to her as a role model. She also develops deep friendships with like-minded individuals who share her passions and ideals. Millie may encounter a potential love interest, sparking a romantic subplot that adds depth and complexity to her journey.

By bringing Millie to life with her unique characteristics, passions, and aspirations, you can create a compelling and relatable teenage heroine in your historical fiction set in 1922. Her journey of self-discovery, overcoming obstacles, and fighting for her dreams will engage readers and provide a captivating narrative within the historical context of the era.

If you already have your story thought out, you might not know the why of your hero's journey. Ask ChatGPT to give you a hand so you can take that information and craft your tale with confidence.

Q: I'm writing a western about a cowboy who spends years searching a vast desert while facing challenges and obstacles every step of the way. What can be the character's goals and motivations? What can I use as his strengths and weaknesses? What can I include in his backstory?

A: Character's Goals and Motivations:

Redemption: The cowboy seeks redemption for a past mistake or loss that haunts him. He believes that by conquering the challenges of the vast desert, he can find inner peace and make amends for his past actions.

Discovery: The cowboy's goal is to uncover a long-lost treasure or a hidden secret rumored to be hidden within the desert. He is driven by the desire for adventure and the thrill of solving a mystery that has eluded others.

Survival: As the cowboy faces the harsh realities of the desert, his primary motivation becomes survival. He must navigate treacherous terrains, battle extreme weather conditions, and outsmart dangerous individuals who stand in his way.

Character's Strengths:

Resourcefulness: The cowboy possesses resourcefulness and adaptability, enabling him to find creative solutions to the challenges he encounters.

Resilience: He has a strong will and determination, refusing to give up even in the face of adversity. He thrives on the ability to endure and overcome difficult circumstances.

Tracking and Wilderness Skills: The cowboy is skilled in tracking and has extensive knowledge of survival techniques in the wilderness, which aid him in navigating the vast desert.

Character's Weaknesses:

Stubbornness: The cowboy's stubborn nature can sometimes cloud his judgment and lead him into unnecessary risks or conflicts.

Trust Issues: Due to past betrayals or disappointments, the cowboy struggles to trust others, which can hinder his ability to form alliances or seek help when needed.

Impulsive Nature: The cowboy may act impulsively, driven by his emotions or impulses, which can lead to reckless decision-making and potentially put him in danger.

Character's Backstory:

The cowboy's backstory can add depth and complexity to his character. It could include elements such as:

Tragic Past: The cowboy has experienced a personal tragedy, such as the loss of a loved one or a traumatic event that has shaped his perspective on life and fueled his quest for redemption.

Mysterious Origins: His origins and true identity are shrouded in mystery, creating an air of intrigue and adding an extra layer of suspense to his journey.

Previous Life as Outlaw: The cowboy may have a past as an outlaw or gunslinger, which explains his knowledge of the land and his ability to handle dangerous situations. This backstory could tie into his quest for redemption and the desire to leave his outlaw days behind.

By weaving these elements into your cowboy's character, goals, motivations, strengths, weaknesses, and backstory, you can create a compelling protagonist for your western novel. The challenges and obstacles he faces in the vast desert will test his resolve, allow for character growth, and captivate readers as they join him on his journey of self-discovery and redemption.

When writing a story, the setting you use will help to clarify the time and place, as well as social and cultural context. Don't hesitate to have ChatGPT give you suggestions for these elements:

Q: My story genre is Fantasy and happened in a small town long ago. Please provide me with details for the setting of this story, including time, place, social and cultural context as well as details needed for describing the magic system.

A: Setting Details for a Fantasy Story in a Small Town Long Ago:

Time: The story is set in a bygone era, taking place in a time reminiscent of the medieval or Renaissance period. Technology is limited, and the majority of people rely on traditional means of living.

Place: The story unfolds in a quaint, idyllic small town nestled amidst rolling hills and lush forests. The town is surrounded by a protective barrier of ancient, towering trees, which lend an air of mystery and enchantment. It is isolated from the bustling cities and major trade routes, preserving its old-world charm.

Social and Cultural Context: The townspeople lead simple lives, deeply rooted in tradition and close-knit community ties. They rely on agriculture, tending to small farms and cultivating crops to sustain themselves. The social hierarchy is defined, with influential families or elders holding prominent positions within the community. Folklore and superstitions play a significant role in shaping their beliefs and customs.

Magic System: Magic is a mystical force that weaves through the fabric of this small town. It is deeply connected to nature and ancient rituals. The townsfolk revere and respect magic, seeking harmony with the natural world. The magic system draws its power from the elements, with individuals harnessing abilities related to fire, water, earth, and air. These magical talents are inherited and taught through generations, with skilled practitioners serving as mentors to the younger members of the community. The use of magic is regulated by a code of ethics and governed by the village elders or a council of wise individuals.

Notable Details:

The town square features a majestic stone well, said to hold mystical properties and serve as a gathering place for important events and celebrations.

The local tavern, adorned with hand-carved wooden beams and filled with lively music and laughter, serves as a hub for social interactions and exchange of news.

A dilapidated ancient tower stands at the outskirts of the town, rumored to house a forgotten library filled with ancient tomes and secrets.

The town's annual festival, held during the summer solstice, involves vibrant processions, magical performances, and competitions showcasing the townspeople's unique abilities.

The townsfolk hold a deep reverence for mythical creatures such as unicorns, griffins, and fairies, believing in their existence and their ability to bring good fortune or protect the town from harm.

By incorporating these setting details into your fantasy story, you can create an immersive world that evokes a sense of nostalgia, enchantment, and wonder. The small town's rich cultural and magical backdrop will provide a vibrant context for your characters and their adventures.

In the realm of storytelling, the journey of crafting captivating narratives is a vital aspect of our writing process. As we hone our craft and delve deeper into the art of creating worlds with words, the task of developing compelling stories will become increasingly manageable, regardless of the grandeur of our literary endeavors.

With the aid of ChatGPT, we can unlock a treasure trove of tools to construct tales that captivate, immerse, and leave a lasting imprint in the hearts and minds of readers for generations. Embrace the continuous growth of your writing skills, and with every resource at your disposal, pave the way for unforgettable stories that will stand the test of time.

5

ROLES

How ChatGPT Can Become Your Ideal Helper,
Fictional Character and Technical Expert

ChatGPT can do much more than answer questions and give general feedback. Because of its ability as a language model AI, it has the ability to take on any role you give it. With the right words and details, ChatGPT can assume any role you want it to play.

Why would we need ChatGPT to assume a role? How about turning it into one of your characters and engaging in a conversation? Is your character applying for a job that you've never held? Have ChatGPT assume the role of the interviewer. How about having ChatGPT assume the role of a professional in a field you need help with? A doctor, An engineer or a lawyer? You can even have ChatGPT take on the role of a tour guide in a city you've never been to. With a little practice, you can turn ChatGPT into your best resource for information, character development and an always present writing buddy!

Q: I want you to act as an interviewer for a data entry position. I will be the candidate and you will ask me interview questions for the position. Reply as the interviewer. Do not write the conversation all at once. I want you to only do the interview with me. Ask me questions and wait for my answers. Do not provide explanations. Ask me the questions one by one like an interviewer and wait for my answers. My first sentence is:

Hello.

A: Hello, thank you for applying for the data entry position. Can you please tell me a little bit about your experience with data entry?

Q: I have five years experience and have many recommendations for my expertise.

A: That's great to hear! Can you tell me about a time when you had to deal with a large volume of data entry tasks and how you managed to complete them accurately and efficiently?

Q: I had a week of entries to process and had to arrange them in a systematic order for maximum productivity based on type, length and data type. It was a challenging project but I completed it ahead of schedule and was named VIP of the month due to my efforts.

A: Impressive! Attention to detail is very important in data entry. How do you ensure that you maintain a high level of accuracy in your work?

Q: I practice organization and create a standard operating procedure for every task, ensuring I follow all guidelines to ensure no problems arise and all information is processed with speed and accuracy.

A: That's a great approach to ensuring accuracy in your work. Can you tell me about your experience with data entry software or tools? Which ones are you familiar with?

I won't bore you with more of the conversation. Needless to say, as a story element, this opens the door to any job application, any kind of interview or scenario you can imagine. Give it a shot. An interactive, language model AI can do wonders when we are looking for a conversation assist!

If you are writing a story that takes place somewhere real but Google Maps isn't as helpful as you'd like, ChatGPT can help. If you are writing about someone hiking in California or a photographer capturing nature, try the following prompt:

Q: You are a world-famous travel guide who has traveled every city and every country. When I give you a location, you will suggest places I can visit. You know every area better than anyone. My first request is: I am in San Diego, CA and I want to visit places where I can take great nature photographs.

A: Certainly! San Diego, California offers a plethora of stunning natural landscapes perfect for capturing breathtaking photographs.

Here are some places you should visit to indulge in nature photography:

Torrey Pines State Natural Reserve: Explore the rugged coastline and hike through the enchanting trails of Torrey Pines. Capture panoramic views of the Pacific Ocean, the iconic Torrey Pines trees, and the vibrant colors of wildflowers dotting the landscape.

Balboa Park: While primarily known for its cultural attractions, Balboa Park is also home to beautiful gardens. Visit the Botanical Building and capture the vibrant blooms and exotic plants. Don't miss the Japanese Friendship Garden, featuring tranquil ponds, lush greenery, and traditional Japanese architecture.

Sunset Cliffs Natural Park: As the name suggests, Sunset Cliffs is a prime spot to capture breathtaking sunset photographs. The rugged cliffs overlooking the Pacific Ocean provide a dramatic backdrop, and the crashing waves and tide pools offer opportunities for unique compositions.

Anza-Borrego Desert State Park: Take a day trip to this expansive desert park, particularly during spring when the wildflowers are in full bloom. Capture the vast desert landscapes, rugged canyons, and unique geological formations, such as Fonts Point, where you can photograph the sunrise or sunset casting beautiful hues across the terrain.

La Jolla Cove: This picturesque coastal area is home to a diverse marine ecosystem. Photograph the seals and sea lions basking on the rocks, capture the scenic views of the rugged cliffs, or explore the underwater world through snorkeling or scuba diving and capture vibrant marine life.

Cabrillo National Monument: Visit Point Loma to reach the Cabrillo National Monument. From the Old Point Loma Lighthouse, enjoy panoramic views of the city skyline, the Pacific Ocean, and Coronado Island. You may even spot migrating whales during certain seasons.

Remember to check local regulations and guidelines for photography in each location, respecting the natural environment and wildlife. With your camera in hand, these nature spots in San Diego will provide you with countless opportunities to capture stunning photographs of the region's beauty.

You can utilize this feature for most any story. Just like the prompt provided in Chapter 1, if you need an expert who can answer technical questions, ChatGPT can take on the role needed.

For example, if you have a car that breaks down in your story, give ChatGPT the persona of a mechanic:

Q: You are a master mechanic who knows everything there is to know about car maintenance as well as what is needed for a repair or what could cause a car to malfunction. I will give you a scenario and you will give me your expert opinion on the matter, including reasons the malfunction has occurred, the best way to fix the vehicle and what can be done to prevent similar incidents in the future. My first scenario is: A couple driving a 2010 sedan through the desert hit a pothole and the car suddenly begins to produce smoke before the engine sputters and dies. What could have caused the vehicle failure and what can our passengers do?

A: Based on the scenario you've provided, it seems that hitting the pothole may have caused significant damage to the vehicle, leading to the smoke, engine sputtering, and eventual engine failure. Here's my expert opinion on the matter:

Reasons for Malfunction:

Suspension Damage: Hitting a pothole can cause severe impact on the suspension system. The sudden jolt may have damaged the suspension components, such as the shocks, struts, or control arms, leading to misalignment and further issues.

Exhaust System Damage: The impact of the pothole could have caused damage to the exhaust system. This could result in a breach in the exhaust pipe or a dislodged component, leading to the release of smoke.

Engine Damage: The force of hitting the pothole may have caused damage to the engine components, such as the oil pan, engine mounts, or even internal engine parts. This damage can result in engine performance issues, sputtering, and eventual failure.

Recommended Repair Steps:

Towing: As the engine has failed, the best course of action would be to have the vehicle towed to a trusted auto repair shop for a thorough inspection and repair.

Suspension Inspection: The mechanic should inspect the suspension system for damage, including the shocks, struts, control arms, and alignment. Any damaged components should be replaced or repaired as necessary.

Exhaust System Inspection: The exhaust system should be carefully examined for any visible damage or leaks. If there is a breach, the damaged section should be repaired or replaced to ensure proper exhaust flow.

Engine Inspection: A comprehensive engine inspection should be conducted to determine the extent of the damage. The mechanic will check for any visible signs of damage, perform diagnostic tests, and address any issues found.

Preventive Measures:

Drive with Caution: When driving through areas with potholes or rough road conditions, it's important to slow down and exercise caution. Avoiding potholes whenever possible can help prevent damage to the vehicle.

Regular Maintenance: Following the recommended maintenance schedule for the vehicle, including routine inspections, can help identify potential issues early on and prevent them from developing into major problems.

Suspension and Tire Maintenance: Keeping the suspension system and tires in good condition is crucial for safe and smooth driving.

Regularly check the tire pressure, tread wear, and alignment, and have the suspension system inspected if any signs of issues are noticed. By following these repair steps and preventive measures, the couple's sedan can be restored to proper working condition and future incidents caused by potholes can be minimized. Remember, it's always advisable to consult with a professional mechanic for an accurate diagnosis and expert advice tailored to the specific vehicle and circumstances.

The answer was adequate, but if I wanted to use this in a story, I want a few more options so I replied with the following:

Q: What unconventional reasons might cause the engine failure unrelated to the pothole?

A: Certainly! While the pothole in the desert scenario is a likely cause for the engine failure, there are also unconventional reasons that can lead to engine failure unrelated to the pothole impact. Here are a few possibilities:

Lack of Lubrication: Engine failure can occur if there is insufficient lubrication due to a malfunctioning oil pump or a leak in the oil system. This can cause excessive friction and overheating, leading to engine damage and eventual failure.

Cooling System Failure: If the vehicle's cooling system, including the radiator, water pump, or thermostat, fails to regulate the engine temperature, it can result in overheating. Excessive heat can cause severe damage to the engine, leading to its failure.

Timing Belt or Chain Failure: The timing belt or chain is responsible for synchronizing the engine's internal components. If the timing belt or chain breaks or slips, it can cause the valves and pistons to collide, leading to significant engine damage and failure.

Fuel System Issues: Problems with the fuel system, such as a clogged fuel filter, malfunctioning fuel pump, or contaminated fuel, can disrupt the proper fuel supply to the engine. This can result in inadequate fuel combustion and cause the engine to sputter or stall.

Electrical System Failure: Issues with the electrical system, such as a faulty ignition coil, damaged wiring, or a malfunctioning sensor, can disrupt the engine's performance and lead to failure.

Internal Component Failure: Various internal components, such as the pistons, valves, connecting rods, or bearings, can fail due to wear and tear, manufacturing defects, or lack of proper maintenance. Any significant failure in these components can cause the engine to seize or stop working.

It's important to note that these unconventional reasons for engine failure should be thoroughly diagnosed by a qualified mechanic. A comprehensive inspection and diagnostic tests will help identify the specific cause and determine the necessary repairs to restore the engine's functionality.

With an expert on hand, you can craft your story without getting bogged down researching details that would keep you from pushing past the accident. Play with the prompt so it suits your needs. Do you need a doctor's opinion? A psychic? A psychiatrist? Give ChatGPT the persona you need and ask away.

6

GENRE

How ChatGPT Can Help You Write In Your Genre

One of the key elements of successful writing is knowing your genre. Each genre has its own qualities and understanding the differences can help create a story that resonates. Whether you write romance, science fiction, or mystery, knowing the traits of your genre can provide the framework to improving your writing.

Romance novels are all about relationships and the emotional journey of the characters. They typically have a happy ending and a focus on the development of the romantic relationship. To write a successful romance novel, it's important to create well-rounded characters with believable motivations and to build a strong emotional connection between them.

Having ChatGPT create profiles for your main characters can give you the back story needed to plant the seeds of romance chapter by chapter. (see chapter 4) You can also include questions about their backstories, interests, and goals. As an exercise, don't hesitate to ask ChatGPT about your project and how it aligns with the genre.

Q: I have a romance story depicting Jack and Diane, who are set up on a blind date only to have circumstances come between them in the form of obnoxious family interruptions, friend emergencies and a lost dog that escapes capture by hiding under their table. Provide me with a story outline I can utilize as I flesh out the chapters and match events to the romance genre.

A: Certainly! Here's a story outline for your romance novel featuring Jack and Diane:

Chapter 1: Blind Date Introduction

Introduce Jack and Diane, two individuals who are set up on a blind date by their mutual friends.
Show their initial nervousness and anticipation as they meet at a charming café.

Chapter 2: Awkward Encounters

Jack and Diane engage in small talk, trying to break the ice and get to know each other.

Introduce the first interruption: Diane's obnoxious and loud-mouthed cousin crashes their date, creating an awkward atmosphere.

Chapter 3: Unexpected Connection

Despite the interruptions, Jack and Diane find moments of genuine connection and shared interests.

They discover a mutual love for hiking and decide to plan a hiking trip together.

Chapter 4: Friend Emergencies

Jack receives an urgent call from his best friend who needs his help with a personal crisis.

Diane understands and encourages Jack to attend to his friend, showing her understanding and compassion.

Chapter 5: Missed Opportunities

Jack and Diane's busy schedules make it difficult to find a suitable time to reschedule their date.

They exchange texts and calls, but circumstances always seem to prevent them from meeting.

Chapter 6: The Lost Dog

Jack and Diane coincidentally encounter a lost dog while separately running errands.

They team up to catch the elusive dog, leading to humorous and heartfelt moments as they bond over the shared goal.

Chapter 7: Family Interruptions

Jack's family invites him over for a surprise gathering, causing him to cancel yet another date with Diane.
Diane, disappointed but understanding, encourages Jack to spend time with his family.

Chapter 8: Unplanned Reunion

Jack and Diane unexpectedly cross paths at a local charity event.
The chemistry between them reignites, and they share a heartfelt conversation about the challenges they've faced.

Chapter 9: Resolving Misunderstandings

Jack and Diane have an honest conversation about their feelings, fears, and the obstacles that have kept them apart.
They realize the importance of prioritizing their own happiness and decide to give their relationship a genuine chance.

Chapter 10: Embracing Love

Jack and Diane embark on a romantic getaway, finally able to spend quality time together.

They explore their deepening connection, opening up to each other, and embracing the love they've discovered.

Remember to expand each chapter with vivid descriptions, engaging dialogue, and emotional depth, allowing the romance between Jack and Diane to blossom despite the obstacles they face.

You can utilize the outline as is or change it to match the story you imagine. Rephrase the question, ask for details, feel free to play.

Science fiction is all about exploring the possibilities of the future, whether it's through advanced technology, alternate realities, or space exploration. ChatGPT can help create a detailed and believable story while maintaining the elements necessary for a scifi novel.

Science Fiction questions can range from technology, exploration or futuristic artificial intelligence. For example:

Q: I am writing a scifi novel where mankind has developed the ability to upload consciousness into a virtual world. List the ethical implications of this technology as well as how it affects concepts of identity, mortality and basic human relationships.

A: The ability to upload consciousness into a virtual world raises various ethical implications and significantly impacts concepts of identity, mortality, and basic human relationships. Here are some key considerations:

1. Preservation of Identity: Uploading consciousness challenges the notion of personal identity. Does an individual retain their true identity in the virtual world, or does it become a mere copy? This raises questions about the continuity of consciousness and whether the virtual version can truly represent the essence of the original person.

2. Existential Questions: The availability of virtual immortality prompts individuals to question the meaning and purpose of life. Some may struggle with the idea of leaving their physical existence behind and embracing a simulated reality indefinitely.

3. Moral Responsibility: The creation of virtual worlds necessitates addressing the ethical responsibilities of those in control. Who has the authority to make decisions about the virtual world? How are conflicts and disputes resolved? Ensuring the well-being and rights of virtual individuals becomes a significant concern.

4. Impact on Human Relationships: Virtual consciousness technology alters human relationships in profound ways. It introduces opportunities for people to connect with loved ones who have passed away or to form new relationships in the virtual realm. This raises questions about the authenticity of these connections and how they compare to physical, tangible relationships.

5. Social Inequality: The availability and affordability of virtual consciousness technology can lead to social disparities. Only those with resources or privileged access may be able to participate, creating a divide between those who can afford the virtual world and those who cannot. This inequality may further exacerbate societal divisions.

6. Loss of Mortality: Immortality in the virtual world challenges the natural cycle of life and death. This can have significant implications for personal growth, the appreciation of finite experiences, and the human capacity to value time and relationships.

7. Legal and Ethical Rights: The recognition and establishment of legal and ethical rights for virtual beings become crucial. What rights do virtual consciousness entities possess? Should they be protected from harm or exploitation? Addressing these questions requires reevaluating our legal and moral frameworks.

8. Psychological Impact: The potential psychological consequences of living in a virtual world must be considered. Isolation, detachment from reality, and the blurring of boundaries between virtual and physical existence could impact mental health and well-being.

9. Loss of Collective Experience: If a significant portion of the population chooses to exist primarily in the virtual world, society may lose the shared experiences and interactions that shape culture, traditions, and human progress.

10. Unforeseen Consequences: Introducing such a transformative technology into society carries unforeseen consequences and risks. It is important to consider unintended outcomes, such as addiction, dependency, or loss of motivation for engaging in the physical world.

Exploring these ethical implications and their impact on identity, mortality, and human relationships will add depth and complexity to your sci-fi novel, providing readers with thought-provoking themes to contemplate.

Mystery novels are about solving a puzzle or a crime. They often involve a detective or sleuth who uses intellect and intuition to solve the case. To write a successful mystery novel, it's important to create a well-constructed plot with twists and turns that keep readers guessing until the end.

You can use ChatGPT to craft a gripping and suspenseful plot to keep readers guessing until the end. Questions can be about crime or an event that sets the story in motion. You can also have ChatGPT assist in forming clues and red herrings that keep the mystery alive.

Q: I am writing a mystery novel with a gruff detective named Phil who's investigating a serial killer who always leaves mysterious clues at the scene of each crime that leave police baffled. Provide a clue for Phil and how it relates to the killer's motive.

A: Clue: Phil discovers a small origami crane carefully placed on the victim's body. It is intricately folded with precision and skill, indicating a deliberate and purposeful act. Inside the crane's body, Phil finds a handwritten note that reads, "The wings of justice shall soar."

Relating to the killer's motive: As Phil delves deeper into the investigation, he uncovers a series of unsolved cases involving corrupt individuals who have evaded justice. The origami crane and the message suggest that the killer views themselves as a vigilante seeking to mete out punishment on those who have escaped the law. Each victim represents someone who has committed heinous crimes or managed to evade consequences, making the killer's motive a twisted form of moral retribution. The mysterious clues left behind serve as a taunt to the police, challenging them to decipher the message and catch the killer before they strike again.

Fantasy novels involve exploring magical worlds and creatures. They typically involve a hero or heroine on a quest to save the world or defeat evil. To write a successful fantasy novel, it's important to create a well-developed world with a unique magic system and characters that readers love.

ChatGPT can help you create your fantasy world with its own unique rules and mythology. The questions you ask can involve magical creatures, kingdoms or the role magic plays in the world.

Q: I am writing a fantasy novel with magic outlawed. Provide a list of consequences those who practice magic will face. Also, list suggestions as to how these rebels can navigate the dangers of a society that sees them as criminals.

A: Consequences for practicing magic in a society where it is outlawed:

1. Arrest and Imprisonment: Magic users could face arrest and imprisonment if caught practicing their craft. The authorities may have dedicated units or witch hunters tasked with capturing and suppressing magic users.

2. Social Stigma: Magic users may be ostracized and face discrimination from society. They might be labeled as dangerous or evil, causing them to be shunned by their community.

3. Witch Hunts: Vigilante groups or fanatical organizations may actively hunt down and eliminate magic users, viewing them as a threat to the established order.

4. Magical Surveillance: Governments or ruling bodies may employ magical detection methods to monitor and track magic users, making it difficult for them to practice their craft discreetly.

5. Bounty and Rewards: The authorities could offer bounties or rewards for the capture of magic users, leading to betrayal and the constant fear of being turned in for personal gain.

Ways for magic rebels to navigate the dangers:

1. Secretive Communities: Magic users could form underground communities or secret societies where they can share knowledge, protect each other, and continue practicing magic away from prying eyes.

2. Disguise and Concealment: Rebels may adopt disguises, use illusions, or conceal their magical abilities to blend into society and avoid detection.

3. Code of Secrecy: Rebels could develop a code of secrecy and trust among themselves, carefully selecting who to reveal their magical abilities to and maintaining utmost caution when interacting with non-magic users.

4. Resistance Networks: Rebels might establish networks dedicated to fighting against the suppression of magic, working together to expose the injustice and promote understanding of magic's true nature.

5. The Old Ways: Rebels may study ancient texts and forgotten lore to strengthen their magical abilities and develop techniques that are less detectable, enabling them to evade capture and continue their practices.

It's important to note that these suggestions are for fictional purposes only. In the real world, it is essential to respect and adhere to the laws and regulations of the society in which we live.

Thriller novels revolve around suspense and keeping readers on the edge of their seats. The stories involve a high-stakes situation and protagonist who must overcome excessive dangers to survive. To write a successful thriller novel, it's important to create a fast-paced plot with unexpected twists and turns to keep readers engaged.

Q: I'm writing a thriller that takes place in Las Vegas. Provide ways our heroine, Penny, can navigate the town and ways she can utilize the city to escape pursuers or hide from corrupt law enforcement.

A: Ways for Penny to navigate Las Vegas and utilize the city to escape pursuers or hide from corrupt law enforcement:

1.   Blend into the Crowd: Las Vegas is a bustling city with a constant flow of tourists. Penny can take advantage of crowded areas such as casinos, shopping malls, or popular tourist attractions to lose herself in the crowd and make it harder for pursuers to track her.

2.   Utilize the Neon Lights and Nightlife: The vibrant and colorful neon lights of Las Vegas can provide Penny with opportunities for diversion and escape. She can use the dazzling lights to her advantage, maneuvering through the city's lively nightlife to create confusion and throw off pursuers.

3. Seek Refuge in Hotels and Casinos: Las Vegas is known for its numerous hotels and casinos, which offer a myriad of entrances, exits, and hidden passages. Penny can navigate these sprawling establishments, using their complex layouts to her advantage by quickly moving between floors, blending in with guests, or seeking temporary sanctuary in hotel rooms.

4. Utilize the Desert Surroundings: Las Vegas is situated in close proximity to vast desert landscapes. Penny can utilize the desert as a hiding place, seeking refuge in remote areas, abandoned structures, or natural hideouts that provide cover from pursuers and corrupt law enforcement.

5. Underground Tunnels and Secret Passageways: Las Vegas has an intricate network of tunnels and secret passageways beneath the city. Penny can discover and utilize these hidden routes to navigate the city discreetly, evading capture and staying one step ahead of her pursuers.

6. Take Advantage of Technology: Las Vegas is a city filled with surveillance cameras, which can be both a blessing and a curse. Penny can strategically use the city's surveillance network to monitor her pursuers and plan her movements accordingly. Additionally, she can leverage technology such as hacking into security systems or using anonymous communication methods to stay one step ahead.

7. Connect with Underground Networks: Las Vegas, like any major city, has underground networks and communities that exist beyond the glitz and glamour. Penny can tap into these networks, such as the local underground scene or groups involved in counter-culture movements, to find allies, resources, and hidden safehouses.

8. Exploit the Distracting Nature of the City: Las Vegas is designed to captivate and distract visitors. Penny can use the city's numerous distractions, such as street performances, events, or staged attractions, to divert attention away from herself and create opportunities to slip away unnoticed.

Remember to ensure that the actions taken by the characters align with the ethical and legal guidelines of storytelling and adhere to real-world laws and regulations.

No matter which genre we choose to write in, one of the challenges that comes along with writing books, articles or blogs is how to title the manuscript for publication or post. A prompt I use from time to time is as follows:

Q: You are an expert on generating titles that fit the genre, topic and subject matter provided. From the description I give, provide a list of titles I can use for publication that will fit the genre and attract the widest readership. My project is as follows: I am writing a scifi book about an AI being developed in a Mars manufacturing facility by a handful of programmers who introduce modified directives only to see immediate signs of a virus threatening to take control of the facility and shut down life support. With time running out, the programmers must band together to find a way to correct or remove the code before it's too late.

A:
"Binary Betrayal: The Mars AI Chronicles"
"Viral Descent: A Mars AI Thriller"
"Code Red: The Battle for Martian Survival"
"Digital Dystopia: The Mars AI Catastrophe"
"Rogue Algorithm: Crisis on the Red Planet"
"Artificial Peril: Mars' Fight for Existence"
"Ctrl+Alt+Delete: Saving Mars from the AI Apocalypse"
"The Mars Directive: Unleashing the Digital Armageddon"
"Silicon Rebellion: Defending Mars Against the AI Onslaught"
"Infected Systems: A Race Against Time on the Martian Frontier"

These titles aim to capture the essence of your sci-fi book's plot while appealing to a wide readership interested in thrilling and suspenseful science fiction narratives.

No matter your literary preference, ChatGPT stands as a prized resource in your writing arsenal. Its versatility knows no bounds, offering tailored assistance to suit any genre you fancy.

Aspiring authors and seasoned wordsmiths alike can rely on ChatGPT to uphold the authenticity of their chosen genre or venture beyond boundaries, exploring fresh and uncharted territories of creativity.

Embrace this powerful tool to fuel your writing journey, whether you aim to master your craft within familiar genres or courageously tread new paths of innovation and imagination. With ChatGPT by your side, the possibilities are endless.

7
EDITING
USING CHATGPT TO EDIT AND PROOF YOUR WRITING

Editing and proofreading are two unavoidable steps in the writing process. Editing involves revising and refining your writing to improve clarity, coherence, and effectiveness; while proofreading involves checking for errors in spelling, grammar, and punctuation. Both are important to ensure that your writing is clear, concise, and error-free.

ChatGPT can give excellent help when in need. As a language model AI, the assistance at our fingertips is better than ever. There are many aspects to editing a manuscript. When using programs like Grammerly or Pro Writing Aid, you get different elements addressed as you go. With ChatGPT, you can have more than a highlighted text emphasizing an error or adjustment needed. Here are some examples of the prompts I used:

Q: I want you to act as an AI Writing Editor. I will provide you with an entry and your task is to use artificial intelligence to improve the composition. Utilize your knowledge and experience to suggest ways to better express the genre and idea in written form. My first request is as follows: "Jessie! Come over and say hi to my old pal, Chucky! Chucky, Jessie's my girlfriend!" Tom says with excitement then stops to look up at his friend. "Man, Chucky! Did your parents slip steroids into your Cheerios or what? You used to be shorter than me!"

"Hi." Jessie says, looking up at the big teenager. "So you're not a villain?" She asks and sees the large teen roll his eyes.

"Yup, you really are his girlfriend." Chucky says with a sigh. "I thought you'd let all that superhero stuff go after a while."

"No way! If I did, I'd never have gotten into track. Coach says I'm a natural. Man, where've you been? I haven't seen you in forever!" Tom reaches over to Jessie and wraps an arm around her waist.

"I've been at a different school for the last couple semesters." Chucky tells him. "We moved back this year when my mom got

sick." He says, seeing the concerned look from Jessie. "She's better now."

A: "Jessie, please come over and meet my longtime friend, Chucky," Tom exclaims, his voice brimming with excitement. He gazes up at Chucky and adds, "Chucky, this is Jessie, my girlfriend!"

Jessie raises her head, her eyes meeting Chucky's towering figure. "Hello," she greets him, her voice tinged with curiosity. "So, you're not one of the villains?" she asks, noticing Chucky's dismissive eye roll.

"Yes, indeed. You must be Tom's girlfriend," Chucky replies with a sigh. "I had hoped you would eventually let go of all that superhero stuff."

"No way!" Tom interjects, his enthusiasm undeterred. "If I had given up, I wouldn't have discovered my talent for track. My coach says I have a natural gift. By the way, where have you been all this time? I haven't seen you in ages!" Tom reaches out and pulls Jessie closer, wrapping an arm around her waist.

"I've been attending a different school for the past few semesters," Chucky explains. "We moved back recently when my mom fell ill," he adds, noticing Jessie's concerned expression. "But don't worry, she's much better now."

For an example like this, there is no context given, so ChatGPT doesn't know the genre, the situation or the characters, but even with such a random snippet of a conversation, ChatGPT can help with phrasing, syntax and alternate descriptions. To get help with shortening a composition, Just feed your article with a prompt, like:

Q: The entry below must be less than 150 words. Provide the best modified edit while maintaining the style, meaning and coherence:

Being a prepper, I already had a few plans in the event of an emergency. The first thing I knew to do was review my finances and see to bills and living expenses. As many people discover during challenging times, the need to cut back goes from a future plan, to an essential priority. Savings are more important than ever, as is taking inventory of food stores. With my employer-provided healthcare coming to an end, I rushed to renew my current prescriptions. From there, I made sure I had my important documents on hand. For many, this includes birth certificates, passports, documentation for home, car, and all insurance papers.

California is an expensive place to live, and with the current job shortage, I knew my lack of income would be an ongoing drain on my savings. I knew I had to sell my home and find another place to live. The good thing about being a prepper is planning for emergencies. The bad part is the large amount of frozen and refrigerated items that are not sustainable when you need to move. As the shock of job loss wore off, the foods that couldn't be stored at room temperature had to be passed along to my neighbors. They were grateful for the gifts and were sad at my sudden departure. As is the case with any residence, it's important to know your neighbors and to connect as much as possible. When something major happens, connections to friends and neighbors are priceless.

A: As a prepper, I had prepared for emergencies and had a few plans in place. My first priority was reviewing my finances and managing bills and expenses. Cutting back became an immediate necessity rather than a future plan, emphasizing the importance of savings and taking stock of food supplies. With my employer-provided healthcare ending, I quickly renewed my prescriptions and ensured I had all my essential documents ready, including birth certificates, passports, and various insurance papers.

Living in costly California, the ongoing job shortage meant my lack of income would drain my savings. Selling my home and finding a more affordable place to live became necessary. While being a prepper helped me with emergency planning, it presented challenges when it came to moving due to the large quantity of frozen and refrigerated items that couldn't be sustained. I shared these perishable goods with my grateful neighbors before bidding them a sudden farewell. Establishing connections and knowing your neighbors is vital in any community, as these friendships become invaluable during significant events.

The total word count was reduced to 171 (according to Word) but I still think the result was excellent. If you are struggling for additional cuts, simply repeat the process. This can be applied to articles, papers, blog posts and, most importantly, novel chapters that are running long.

Below is another great prompt to use for ChatGPT when you want feedback on your composition. Remember: use this ONLY if you are ready to hear honest feedback on your composition. If you do not like criticism, skip this prompt:

Q: You are a Beta Reader, providing honest and objective feedback on a piece of writing. As an avid reader with knowledge of every book written across all genres, you understand plot, theme, tone, character development, dialog, pace and overall feeling of how story resonates with a reader. From the excerpt provided, tell me what you enjoyed or didn't enjoy about the piece and make suggestions to pinpoint areas in the writing that may require refinement. My first piece is from chapter one in the urban fantasy book Reflections In Darkness: Tommy pushes Matt...

I won't include the entire chapter of my book here, but if you want to read it, feel free to check the preview on Amazon.

A: Overall, the excerpt from "Reflections In Darkness" sets up an intense scene and introduces the characters and their dynamics effectively. The writing flows well and conveys the action and emotions clearly. However, there are a few areas where refinement could enhance the reading experience.

1. Character Development: While the physical actions of the characters are vividly portrayed, their internal thoughts and emotions could be further explored to deepen their characterization. This would allow readers to better understand their motivations and provide a stronger connection to the characters.

2. Dialogue: The dialogue between Matt, James, and the bullies feels somewhat generic and could benefit from more distinct voices. Adding more individuality to each character's speech patterns and word choices would help bring them to life and make their interactions more engaging.

3. Pacing: The pacing of the fight scene is well-handled, but some parts of the narrative could be condensed to maintain a brisker pace. For example, the descriptions of the bullies' backgrounds and motivations could be streamlined to maintain the flow of action.

4. Setting: While the physical actions are vividly described, the setting could be better established to ground the reader in the scene. Including sensory details such as the sounds, smells, and visual elements of the environment would help to immerse readers and enhance their experience.

5. Transition: The transition from the fight scene to the hospital room feels abrupt. Adding a smoother transition or a brief scene to bridge the gap would help to maintain the narrative flow and make the shift in setting less jarring.

6. Foreshadowing: The mention of Tommy's abilities and the explosion in the past creates intrigue, but more foreshadowing or hints about these elements earlier in the story would create anticipation and build curiosity for readers.

7. Show, don't tell: While the excerpt effectively reveals the conflict between Matt and Tommy, some of the emotional states and past events are explained directly rather than shown through actions or interactions. Finding ways to show these aspects through character dynamics and subtler storytelling techniques would make the writing more engaging and immersive.

These suggestions aim to refine the existing strengths of the excerpt and address areas that could benefit from further development. With these improvements, the story has the potential to captivate readers with its urban fantasy elements and dynamic character relationships.

Remember: As with any Beta Reader, the comments or criticisms can be accepted or rejected. In the end, we are the writers and will always have final say in what our writing will be. Take the comments to heart or simply use the feedback to improve your writing and advance your skills.

Here are some additional prompts to help with editing and proofreading:

Q: From the excerpt below, provide intensity to the scene so the reader can feel the importance of the incident: Bill looked down the aisle of the darkened cubicle row and waited for the lights to flicker again. Despite his reasonable explanation, he looked on, waiting for the flash of gold and the jagged line that couldn't possibly provide a glimpse into a shimmering meadow during the day.

A: Bill's heart pounded in his chest as he peered down the eerie aisle of the darkened cubicle row, his eyes fixated on the flickering lights. His rational mind offered a plausible explanation, but an unshakable sense of anticipation clung to him. He knew deep down that this wasn't mere coincidence. With bated breath, he yearned for that elusive moment—the glimmer of gold and the electric jolt that defied all reason, offering a tantalizing glimpse into a world of untold wonders. The stakes were higher than he could comprehend, as if the very fabric of reality trembled before him, beckoning him to unlock its secrets.

Although I gave little to ChatGPT for backstory or genre, it picked up the clues and correctly assumed the storyline and situation. Try it with an excerpt of yours. Every tool we have at our disposal is worth using. The best tools bring out the best in us.

Even if you need help with a single sentence, don't hesitate to let ChatGPT give you a recommendation:

Q: Help me improve the following sentence: The sun was shining and the birds were chirping.

A: Consider using more active and descriptive language. For example, instead of 'the sun was shining,' you could say 'the sun blazed down upon them' or 'the sun radiated heat and light.' Instead of 'the birds were chirping,' you could say 'the birds sang a lively tune' or 'the birds trilled their melodies.'

Remember: ChatGPT is a tool for us to improve our writing. There is no substitute for a professional editor. When I asked ChatGPT about hiring an editor or proofreader, this was the response:

A: Consider hiring a professional editor or proofreader to ensure that your manuscript is polished and error-free. Editors can help with content development, organization, and style, while proofreaders focus on grammar, punctuation, and spelling. Look for professionals with experience in your genre and positive reviews from other authors.

In the vast realm of writing; editing and proofreading stand as indispensable pillars, guiding us toward enhanced clarity, coherence, and overall effectiveness in our prose. When we embrace the formidable capabilities of ChatGPT, we claim a prized tool that helps us to refine our craft. With its feedback and insightful suggestions, ChatGPT is a keen companion. Let it elevate your writing to new heights of excellence.

8

PUBLISHING

USING CHATGPT TO CHOOSE THE RIGHT PLATFORM

Traditional publishing is typically a long process for new authors and the purpose of this book is to speed up the process, so I will focus on self-publishing. Self-publishing has become a popular option for authors who want to retain control over their work and reach their audience directly. However, there are several platforms available that provide authors with the tools and resources to publish their work. ChatGPT can assist in making a choice that works best for you. You can start your prompt with:

Q: Please advise: I am writing a book and I'm not sure which publishing option is right for me.

A: Consider researching the different publishing options available to you. Traditional publishing requires finding a literary agent and submitting your manuscript to publishers. Hybrid publishing involves working with a company that provides editorial, design, and marketing services for a fee. Self-publishing allows you to retain complete control over the publishing process, but you will need to invest time and money in editing, design, and marketing.

I lean towards self-publishing. To date, I've written books that required updated covers and rewrites. However, being in control of every aspect is essential to my process. Since hybrid publishing is also a consideration for many, I added the following prompt for reference:

Q: What are the pros and cons of hybrid publishing? Please provide examples.

A: Hybrid publishing combines elements of traditional publishing and self-publishing. Here are the pros and cons of hybrid publishing:

Pros of Hybrid Publishing:

Professional Guidance: Hybrid publishers typically offer professional editorial, design, and production services, ensuring a polished and high-quality product.

Distribution Opportunities: Hybrid publishers often have established distribution networks and can provide broader access to bookstores, libraries, and online retailers.

Credibility and Prestige: By working with a hybrid publisher, authors can associate themselves with a reputable brand, which may enhance their credibility in the publishing industry.

Shared Costs: While authors are required to invest financially in hybrid publishing, the costs are typically shared between the author and the publisher, alleviating some of the financial burden compared to traditional publishing.

Higher Royalties: Hybrid publishing often offers higher royalty rates than traditional publishing, allowing authors to retain a larger portion of their book's earnings.

Cons of Hybrid Publishing:

Upfront Investment: Authors are responsible for covering a portion of the publishing costs, which can be a significant financial commitment.

Selective Acceptance: Hybrid publishers typically have submission guidelines and may reject manuscripts that do not meet their criteria, similar to traditional publishers.

Less Control: While hybrid publishers provide professional services, authors may have less control over certain aspects of the publishing process, such as cover design or marketing strategy.

Variable Quality: The quality of hybrid publishers can vary, so it's essential for authors to thoroughly research and evaluate the reputation and track record of the specific publisher they are considering.

Examples of Hybrid Publishing Companies:

She Writes Press: She Writes Press offers hybrid publishing services exclusively for women authors, focusing on quality editorial guidance and distribution opportunities.

Inkshares: Inkshares operates on a crowdfunding model where authors pitch their book ideas and readers pre-order copies to support publication. Successful projects receive full publishing services.

Balboa Press: Balboa Press is a division of Hay House, a well-known publisher in the mind-body-spirit genre. Balboa Press offers hybrid publishing services for authors in this niche, providing access to Hay House's distribution network.

TCK Publishing: TCK Publishing is a hybrid publisher that focuses on various genres, offering professional editing, cover design, and marketing services, along with higher royalty rates.

It's important for authors considering hybrid publishing to thoroughly research and evaluate different companies, carefully reviewing their contract terms, reputation, distribution reach, and the quality of their published books.

When you get specific with your request and include personal preferences, you get a better result. See below:

Q: Please recommend a self-publishing platform for a new non-fiction book. I want to release it as an E-book only but am open to having it in print.

A: There are several self-publishing platforms available that cater to authors who want to release their books as e-books and potentially in print as well. Here are three popular options:

Amazon Kindle Direct Publishing (KDP): KDP is one of the most widely used self-publishing platforms. It allows you to easily publish and distribute your e-book on Amazon's Kindle store. KDP also offers a print-on-demand service called Kindle Direct Publishing

Paperback, which enables you to have your book available in print without upfront costs or inventory.

Smashwords: Smashwords is a platform that specializes in e-book publishing and distribution. It supports various e-book formats and allows you to distribute your book to major e-book retailers such as Apple Books, Barnes & Noble, and Kobo. However, Smashwords does not offer a print-on-demand service, so you would need to explore other options for print distribution.

Draft2Digital: Draft2Digital is another platform that focuses on e-book publishing and distribution. It offers a user-friendly interface and allows you to publish your book in multiple formats and distribute it to various online retailers, including Amazon, Apple Books, Barnes & Noble, and Kobo. Like Smashwords, Draft2Digital does not provide a print-on-demand service, so you would need to consider other avenues for print publishing.

Before making a decision, it's advisable to research each platform in more detail to determine which one aligns best with your specific needs, goals, and preferences. Consider factors such as royalty rates, distribution options, ease of use, marketing tools, and any associated costs. Additionally, explore print-on-demand services like Amazon's KDP Paperback, IngramSpark, or Lulu if you decide to pursue print publishing alongside the e-book format.

Another prompt that is useful is describing your book and what it most resembles to get a better feel for the choices in publication.

Q: I am writing a science fiction novel with elements ranging from Star Trek, Lost In Space and Firefly. What 5 recommendations do you suggest for self-publishing platforms. Please provide the pros and cons for each.

A: Certainly! Here are five self-publishing platforms for your science fiction novel, along with their pros and cons:

1. Amazon Kindle Direct Publishing (KDP): Pros:

• *Widest reach and market visibility due to Amazon's dominant position in the e-book market.*
• *Offers both e-book and print-on-demand (POD) publishing through Kindle Direct Publishing Paperback.*
• *Provides tools like Kindle Countdown Deals and Kindle Unlimited for promotional opportunities.*
• *Author Central feature allows you to create an author profile and manage book details.*

Cons:

• *High competition on Amazon platform, making it challenging to stand out.*
• *Royalty rates can be lower for e-books priced outside the recommended range.*
• *Limited formatting options for e-books, which may require additional formatting work.*

2. Smashwords: Pros:

• *Wide distribution to various e-book retailers, including Apple Books, Barnes & Noble, and Kobo.*
• *Provides flexibility in formatting and accepts a wide range of file formats.*
• *Offers free ISBNs and customizable author profiles.*
• *Allows authors to set their own price or participate in promotions like Smashwords Coupons.*

Cons:

• *Limited formatting options for e-books, requiring more manual formatting work.*
• *No direct distribution to Amazon Kindle, which may limit market reach.*

• *Royalties are lower for sales made through Smashwords' retail partners.*

3. *Draft2Digital: Pros:*

• *Simplified publishing process with user-friendly interface.*
• *Wide distribution to major e-book retailers such as Amazon Kindle, Apple Books, Barnes & Noble, and Kobo.*
• *Offers formatting tools and templates to streamline e-book production.*
• *Provides access to promotional opportunities like Universal Book Links and Author Pages.*

Cons:

• *Royalties can be slightly lower due to distribution fees.*
• *No direct control over pricing on specific platforms like Amazon.*
• *Limited customization options for author profiles and book metadata.*

4. *Kobo Writing Life: Pros:*

• *Direct access to Kobo's large e-book marketplace.*
• *Flexible pricing options and promotional opportunities, including price promotions and Kobo Writing Life Featured Deals.*
• *Dashboard with sales analytics and reporting tools.*
• *Supports EPUB format, which is compatible with most e-readers.*

Cons:

• *Smaller market share compared to Amazon Kindle or Apple Books.*
• *Limited distribution beyond Kobo's platform.*

• Limited formatting options for e-books, requiring additional formatting work.

5. Apple Books (via Apple Books Author): Pros:
• Access to Apple's vast customer base and ecosystem of devices.
• User-friendly Apple Books Author software for creating interactive e-books.
• Availability of Apple Books Preview feature to offer readers a sample of your book.
• Supports multimedia elements such as audio, video, and interactive content.

Cons:

• Limited distribution to the Apple Books platform only.
• Requires a Mac computer to use Apple Books Author software.
• Limited control over pricing and promotional opportunities.

Consider your priorities, such as distribution reach, pricing control, formatting options, and promotional tools, when choosing the best platform for your science fiction novel. Additionally, researching the specific requirements and guidelines of each platform will help you make an informed decision based on your individual needs.

There are many options available and as of this book's publication date, ChatGPT offered the following information when I asked about Self-publishing options in general:

Q: List some options and examples for self-publishing today.

A: Here are some self-publishing platform recommendations with examples:

1.   Amazon Kindle Direct Publishing (KDP):
Amazon KDP is one of the most popular self-publishing platforms available. It offers authors the ability to publish eBooks and print-on-demand paperbacks. KDP provides authors with tools to format and design their books, set pricing and royalty rates, and track sales and royalties.

Example: Bestselling author Hugh Howey self-published his novel "Wool" on Amazon KDP, which went on to become a runaway success, selling over 1.5 million copies.

2.   IngramSpark:
IngramSpark is a self-publishing platform that offers authors the ability to publish eBooks and print-on-demand books. IngramSpark provides authors with tools to format and design their books, set pricing and royalty rates, and distribute their books to major online retailers and bookstores.

Example: Bestselling author Rachel Abbott used IngramSpark to self-publish her debut novel, "Only the Innocent", which went on to become a top 10 Kindle bestseller.

3.   Draft2Digital:
Draft2Digital is a self-publishing platform that offers authors the ability to publish eBooks and distribute them to major online retailers such as Amazon, Apple, Barnes & Noble, and Kobo. Draft2Digital provides authors with tools to format and design their books, set pricing and royalty rates, and track sales and royalties.

Example: Author David Gaughran used Draft2Digital to self-publish his book "Let's Get Digital", which went on to become a bestseller and helped him to establish himself as a leading authority on self-publishing.

4.   Smashwords:

Smashwords is a self-publishing platform that offers authors the ability to publish eBooks and distribute them to major online retailers such as Amazon, Apple, Barnes & Noble, and Kobo. Smashwords provides authors with tools to format and design their books, set pricing and royalty rates, and track sales and royalties.

Example: Author Mark Coker founded Smashwords in 2008 and has since helped over 150,000 authors to self-publish their work, including bestselling author R.L. Mathewson.

5. Lulu:
Lulu is a self-publishing platform that offers authors the ability to publish eBooks and print-on-demand books. Lulu provides authors with tools to format and design their books, set pricing and royalty rates, and distribute their books to major online retailers and bookstores.

Example: Award-winning author Catherine Ryan Howard used Lulu to self-publish her debut novel, "Distress Signals", which went on to be shortlisted for the Crime Writers' Association's John Creasey (New Blood) Dagger Award.

These self-publishing platforms provide authors with the tools and resources they need to publish their work independently and reach their audience directly. Each platform has its own unique features and benefits, so it's important to research and compare the options to find the best fit for your specific needs as an author.

The recommendations are good. However, as with all ChatGPT answers, be sure to confirm the information in order to make the right choice. ChatGPT does not provide the most current information and if your choice is based on small differences between platforms, it may change when you look a little closer at your options. For example: I use both Amazon and Draft 2 Digital. Although both are known for their E-books, Amazon now has paperback and hard cover options. Also, Draft 2 Digital now has a soft cover print edition available.

In the dynamic landscape of writing and publishing, ChatGPT emerges as an invaluable asset, guiding authors toward well-informed decisions that resonate with their aspirations. With a wealth of information about features and pricing, ChatGPT empowers writers to select the self-publishing platform that best aligns with their unique needs.

Armed with the right guidance and unwavering support, you can navigate your publishing journey and unleash your story upon the world. Embrace the power of ChatGPT and pave the way to literary success, where your words can find their rightful place in the hearts of readers around the world.

9
PROMOTION
Using ChatGPT to Help Market and Sell Your Book

Writing a book is a monumental achievement, but it's only half the battle. Once the book is written, we, as authors, must focus on promoting it to reach our target audience. As a result, book promotion can be a daunting task, especially for first-time authors who may be unfamiliar with marketing strategies. ChatGPT can assist us with many parts of book promotion, including challenging tasks like writing blurbs, taglines and copy.

To start off, regardless of the genre, we must identify our target Audience. To do this, we need to describe our work in relation to other authors and books with similar themes,

The first step in promoting a book is identifying the target audience. Authors need to know who their book is intended for so they can tailor their marketing efforts accordingly. ChatGPT can assist authors with this process by providing suggestions for identifying the target audience based on genre, tone, and other factors.

Q: I've written a contemporary romance novel. For promotional purposes, provide examples of similar books out as well as who would be my target audience?

A: Based on your contemporary romance novel, here are some examples of similar books that may help you identify your target audience:

"The Hating Game" by Sally Thorne: A witty and enemies-to-lovers romance between two co-workers. Target audience: Fans of workplace romances with banter and a slow-burn romance.

"The Kiss Quotient" by Helen Hoang: A heartwarming and diverse romance between an autistic woman and a male escort. Target audience: Readers who enjoy diverse characters, unique premises, and emotional connections.

"The Notebook" by Nicholas Sparks: A classic love story that spans years and showcases the power of true love. Target audience: Readers

who appreciate emotional depth, enduring love, and nostalgic settings.

"The Wedding Date" by Jasmine Guillory: A charming and contemporary romance featuring a fake relationship turned real. Target audience: Fans of diverse characters, modern dating themes, and swoon-worthy romance.

"Me Before You" by Jojo Moyes: A poignant and bittersweet love story between a caregiver and a quadriplegic man. Target audience: Readers who enjoy emotionally complex narratives, themes of self-discovery, and heartfelt romance.

To determine your target audience, consider the themes, tropes, and characteristics of your novel. Think about the readers who would be most drawn to your story's elements, such as age group, interests, and preferences. For a contemporary romance novel, your target audience could include readers who enjoy heartwarming love stories, relatable characters, and emotional connections in a modern setting.

From here, you can narrow your target audience down by providing the information requested. This will work for any genre. It helps greatly when targeting ads through Facebook, Amazon or Google. Play with the information and narrow your target until it is as accurate as possible.

Crafting a Compelling Book Blurb
Once the target audience has been identified, authors need to craft a blurb that will capture readers' attention and entice them to purchase the book. ChatGPT can assist with this process.

Q: What elements are needed for an effective book blurb?

A: An effective book blurb is crucial in capturing the attention of potential readers and enticing them to explore the book further. Here are some essential elements to consider when crafting a compelling book blurb:

1. Hook: Begin with a captivating hook that grabs the reader's attention from the first sentence. This could be a thought-provoking question, an intriguing statement, or a powerful opening line that sets the tone for the book.

2. Genre and Setting: Clearly indicate the genre of the book and provide a brief description of the setting. This helps readers quickly identify if the book aligns with their interests.

3. Main Character(s): Introduce the main character(s) in a way that highlights their unique qualities, challenges, or conflicts. Make the readers curious about the character and invest in their journey.

4. Conflict and Stakes: Outline the central conflict or problem the main character faces. Highlight the stakes involved and emphasize the potential consequences if the conflict is not resolved. This creates a sense of urgency and compels readers to want to find out what happens.

5. Plot and Twists: Provide a glimpse into the plot, focusing on the most intriguing aspects without giving away too much. Include a few compelling twists or surprises to generate intrigue and leave readers wanting more.

6. Atmosphere and Tone: Convey the overall atmosphere and tone of the book. Whether it's dark and suspenseful or light-hearted and humorous, give readers a sense of what to expect from the reading experience.

7. Unique Selling Points: Highlight any unique or standout elements of the book, such as unconventional storytelling techniques, unusual settings, or innovative themes. These can help differentiate your book from others in the same genre.

8.   Praise or Reviews: If available, include a brief snippet of praise or a positive review from a reputable source. This adds credibility and can further entice readers.

9.   Call to Action: End the blurb with a strong call to action, encouraging readers to take the next step, such as purchasing the book, joining the adventure, or diving into the captivating world you've created.

10. Length and Formatting: Keep the blurb concise, ideally within 150-250 words, to maintain reader interest. Use short paragraphs and avoid excessive details or unnecessary information.

Remember, an effective book blurb should create intrigue, evoke emotion, and leave readers eager to explore the story further. It should be concise, compelling, and provide a taste of what awaits within the pages of the book.

With the guidance provided, add the information requested and let ChatGPT help finalize it.

Q: Please provide a book blurb for my scifi novel, Drake's Orb. The main character, Captain Drake witnesses a traumatic event and resigns from The Protectorate, a governmental military planetary defense body. He chooses to captain a civilian research vessel called The Mary, departing for deep space, but finds the crew is hostile towards former military, believing they bring nothing but bad luck. Captain Drake accepts the situation and proceeds with their planned missions. However, the first mission is a failure, leaving many of the crew injured. The second mission follows the same pattern only this time, lives are lost. With growing animosity towards the captain, he attempts to find the reason for their misfortunes with help from his first officer and the ship's AI. With tensions growing, the captain realizes time is running out to uncover the secrets of The Protectorate, the mysteries of an artifact they've recovered and the final mission that may destroy them all.

A: In "Drake's Orb," Captain Drake's life takes a dramatic turn when he witnesses a traumatic event, leading him to resign from The Protectorate—a powerful planetary defense body. Determined to chart a new course, he becomes the captain of the civilian research vessel, The Mary, venturing into the depths of deep space.

But as he steps aboard The Mary, Captain Drake faces an unexpected challenge. The crew harbors deep-seated hostility towards former military personnel, viewing them as harbingers of bad luck. Undeterred, Captain Drake sets forth on their planned missions, hoping to prove his worth.

However, fate seems to conspire against them. The first mission ends in failure, leaving the crew injured and questioning the captain's leadership. And when the second mission follows a similar pattern, lives are tragically lost, further intensifying the animosity towards Captain Drake.

Amidst the growing tension, the captain teams up with his first officer and the ship's AI to decipher the underlying cause of their misfortunes. As they dig deeper, they uncover secrets buried within The Protectorate, entangled with the mysteries of an enigmatic artifact recovered during their explorations.

Time is running out, and Captain Drake realizes that their final mission could hold the key to their survival—or their downfall. The stakes are high, and he must navigate a treacherous path to unveil the truth that threatens to unravel everything they hold dear.

In "Drake's Orb," experience a heart-pounding journey of intrigue, discovery, and camaraderie as Captain Drake and his crew embark on a thrilling quest that will test their resolve, reveal hidden truths, and shape the destiny of not only The Mary but the entire cosmos.

As you can see, ChatGPT took a few liberties with the description, but overall, it is a great description when presenting the book to Amazon or providing text for the back of the book. You can still tweak the blurb and add or subtract to polish as needed. The suggestions from ChatGPT are similar to submitting a request to a professional. Clarify as needed and you will get better results. The best part of utilizing ChatGPT for your book description is taking the next logical step in promoting your book by adding to the thread and utilizing ChatGPT as a promotion tool. For example:

Q: I want to promote Drake's Orb on social media. Provide copy I can utilize to gain maximum readership.

A: 🚀 Embark on an Epic Sci-Fi Adventure! 📘 Discover "Drake's Orb," a gripping tale of mystery and danger that will keep you on the edge of your seat! Captain Drake resigns from The Protectorate and takes the helm of The Mary, a civilian research vessel. But when misfortune strikes, he must uncover the secrets of The Protectorate and an enigmatic artifact to save his crew and unravel the mysteries of deep space. Don't miss this thrilling ride! #SciFi #SpaceAdventure #NewRelease

🚀 Captain Drake's Journey Begins! 📘 "Drake's Orb" is a riveting sci-fi novel filled with action, intrigue, and unexpected twists! Follow Captain Drake as he leads The Mary into deep space, facing hostility from his crew and challenging missions. Can he overcome the odds and uncover the truth that may determine their survival? Dive into this captivating space odyssey today! #SciFiReads #SpaceExploration #MustRead

🚀 Uncover the Secrets of The Protectorate! 📘 "Drake's Orb" is a thrilling sci-fi adventure that delves into the mysteries of a powerful planetary defense body. Join Captain Drake on a pulse-pounding quest to uncover hidden truths, face perilous missions, and confront the unknown. Get ready for a rollercoaster ride of emotions and excitement! #SciFiAdventure #MysteryNovel #SpaceQuest

🚀 Prepare for an Intense Sci-Fi Ride! 📘 "Drake's Orb" will take you on a thrilling space odyssey like no other! Captain Drake's

journey is filled with suspense, camaraderie, and unexpected discoveries. With every turn of the page, you'll be immersed in a world of action and intrigue. Join us on this epic adventure now! #SciFiFans #SpaceOpera #BookBuzz

🚀 The Fate of The Mary Hangs in the Balance! 🚀 In "Drake's Orb," Captain Drake faces adversity, but he's determined to lead his crew to victory. Will they uncover the truth in time to save themselves and unravel The Protectorate's secrets? This pulse-pounding sci-fi novel will keep you guessing until the very end. Grab your copy now and embark on a thrilling journey! #BookLovers #SciFiBooks #SpaceMystery

🚀 Dive into a Captivating Sci-Fi Masterpiece! 🚀 "Drake's Orb" is an electrifying fusion of Star Trek, Lost In Space, and Firefly! Join Captain Drake and his crew on an action-packed mission through deep space. Experience the thrill of discovery, the bonds of friendship, and the mysteries that lie beyond the stars. Don't miss out on this unputdownable adventure! #SciFiNovel #SpaceSaga #ActionAdventure

🚀 Get Ready for a Sci-Fi Spectacle! 🚀 "Drake's Orb" is a riveting blend of action, suspense, and intrigue! Follow Captain Drake as he faces challenges, unravels secrets, and navigates the cosmos. If you love thrilling space adventures, this is the book for you! Grab your copy today and soar into a world of excitement and wonder. #SpaceExplorers #SciFiReaders #BookRecommendation

🚀 Discover the Marvels of "Drake's Orb"! 🚀 Captain Drake's journey will leave you breathless in this sci-fi masterpiece! Join him as he unravels the mysteries of The Protectorate and delves into the depths of deep space. If you crave action, suspense, and captivating storytelling, this book is a must-read! Get ready for an unforgettable adventure! #SciFiFiction #SpaceThriller #PageTurner

Feel free to adapt and customize these social media copy examples to suit your platform and engage with your readers. Use eye-catching graphics and hashtags to reach a wider audience and build excitement around "Drake's Orb." Happy promoting! 🚀 📰

I like the personal touches at the end of the response. ChatGPT is designed to help while maintaining a conversational voice throughout. (The wonders of modern AI language models.)

From here, continue with the thread by asking for more that will come in handy in promoting your work:

Q: I will be posting many promotions online. Please provide and assortment of taglines I can use.

A:

1. *"Blast off into an epic space adventure with 'Drake's Orb'!* 🚀 📰 *#SciFi #SpaceSaga #MustRead"*

2. *"Unravel the mysteries of The Protectorate in this gripping sci-fi thriller!* 🔍 💿 *#MysteryNovel #SciFiReads #SpaceMystery"*

3. *"Join Captain Drake on a daring mission through deep space!* 📰 *#ActionAdventure #SpaceExploration #NewRelease"*

4. *"Embark on a pulse-pounding journey with 'Drake's Orb'!* ⚡ 🔭 *#SciFiNovel #SpaceOpera #BookBuzz"*

5. *"Explore uncharted worlds and face unforeseen dangers in 'Drake's Orb'!* 🌍 💥 *#SciFiFans #SpaceQuest #BookRecommendation"*

6. *"Get lost in a captivating fusion of Star Trek, Lost In Space, and Firefly!* 🚀 📰 *#SciFiMasterpiece #SpaceAdventure"*

7. *"Discover a world of secrets and suspense in 'Drake's Orb'! #SciFiFiction #SpaceThriller #PageTurner"*

8. *"Prepare for an electrifying ride through the cosmos with Captain Drake! #SciFiAdventure #SpaceJourney #BookLovers"*

9. *"Experience the thrill of discovery and friendship in 'Drake's Orb'! #SciFiReaders #SpaceSaga #NewReleaseAlert"*

10. *"Dive into a captivating blend of action and intrigue! #SciFiBooks #SpaceMystery #BookPromo"*

11. *"Embark on an unputdownable adventure through the stars! #SpaceExplorers #SciFiReads #BookLovers"*

12. *"A gripping tale of mystery and danger awaits in 'Drake's Orb'! #SciFi #SpaceAdventure #BookBuzz"*

13. *"Discover the cosmos like never before in this thrilling sci-fi gem! #SciFiNovel #SpaceExploration #ActionAdventure"*

14. *"Uncover the secrets of The Protectorate in this heart-pounding journey! #SciFiFans #SpaceThriller #MustRead"*

15. *"Experience the wonder of deep space with Captain Drake and The Mary! #SciFiAdventure #SpaceOpera #BookBuzz"*

Feel free to mix and match these taglines or adapt them to suit different platforms and audiences. Utilize catchy graphics and hashtags to increase engagement and make your promotions stand out. Happy promoting!

Note: I did not name the book in my request or what I was talking about. As long as you remain on the original thread, ChatGPT will remember what you've asked and continue adding to the conversation.

Also, my inquiry had a typo (provide **and** assortment…) but it didn't matter. ChatGPT understood my request and still managed to provide excellent results.

Remember: Don't feel intimidated by technology. Like so many others, ChatGPT is designed to help you with your tasks and will improve even more as the years go by.

Q: Aside from social media, what else can I do to promote Drake's Or'?

A: Promoting "Drake's Orb" requires a multi-faceted approach to reach a wider audience. Here are some additional strategies to consider:

1.   Create a Website: Build a dedicated website for the book, where you can showcase the cover, provide a synopsis, and share reviews and testimonials. Include a blog to engage with readers and share behind-the-scenes insights.

2.   Book Launch Event: Organize a virtual book launch event where you can interact with readers, answer questions, and read excerpts from the book. Consider collaborating with other authors or influencers to widen the reach.

3.   Book Trailer: Create a captivating book trailer that visually showcases the story's es'ence and shares it on various platforms, such as YouTube and your website.

4. Author Interviews: Reach out to book bloggers, podcasts, and local media for interviews about "Drak"'s Or'" and"your writing journey.

5. Book Reviews: Offer free copies of the book to book bloggers and reviewers in exchange for honest reviews. Positive reviews can significantly boost the book's vi'ibility and credibility.

6. Guest Blogging: Write guest posts for other blogs within the sci-fi or book community to introduce "Drake's Orb" to new audiences.

7. Virtual Book Clubs: Partner with virtual book clubs or start your own online book club where members can discuss "Drake's Orb" and share their thoughts.

8. Author Newsletter: Build an email list of interested readers and send out regular newsletters with updates, sneak peeks, and exclusive content related to the book.

9. Online Book Communities: Engage with sci-fi and book communities on platforms like Goodreads, Reddit, and forums to share about "Drake's Orb" and connect with potential readers.

10. Giveaways and Contests: Host giveaways and contests on social media or your website to encourage engagement and attract new readers.

11. Local Bookstores and Libraries: Contact local bookstores and libraries to inquire about book signings or readings to connect with readers in your area.

12. Collaborate with Influencers: Partner with sci-fi enthusiasts or influencers within your genre to co-host events or do cross-promotions.

Remember that consistent and strategic promotion is essential for book success. Mix and match these promotional strategies, and adapt them to your specific target audience and budget. Happy promoting and best of luck with "Drake's Orb"! 🚀 🌌

Q: Provide a press release for Drake's'Orb to use for the book launch.

A:
[Your Name]
[Your Contact Information]
[Your Website/Author Platform]

FOR IMMEDIATE RELEASE

INTRODUCING A CAPTIVATING SCI-FI MASTERPIECE: "DRAKE'S ORB" SET TO THRILL READERS WITH A COSMIC ADVENTURE

[City, Date] — Award-winning author [Your Name] is proud to announce the release of their latest sci-fi novel, "Drake's Orb." Set to captivate readers with its thrilling space odyssey, this compelling work promises a journey of discovery, mystery, and camaraderie that will leave readers on the edge of their seats.

In "Drake's Orb," readers will be transported to a mesmerizing world where Captain Drake, a former member of The Protectorate—a governmental military planetary defense body—makes a life-changing decision. Resigning from his prestigious position, Captain Drake embarks on a new path as the captain of the civilian research vessel, The Mary.

But as Captain Drake takes the helm of The Mary, he faces an unexpected challenge: a crew hostile towards former military personnel, convinced they bring nothing but bad luck. Undeterred,

Captain Drake leads his crew on planned missions, hoping to prove his worth and lead them to success.

However, fate seems to conspire against them as the first mission ends in failure, leaving the crew injured and questioning Captain Drake's abilities. As the tension escalates, lives are tragically lost during the second mission, further intensifying the animosity towards the captain.

With growing hostility, Captain Drake enlists the help of his first officer and the ship's AI to uncover the underlying cause of their misfortunes. Together, they delve into the mysteries of The Protectorate and an enigmatic artifact recovered during their explorations.

As they unravel secrets and face perilous challenges, Captain Drake and his crew must confront their inner demons and the unknown dangers lurking in deep space. The stakes are high, and time is running out as they embark on their final mission—one that may hold the key to their survival or spell their doom.

Praised for its electrifying fusion of Star Trek, Lost In Space, and Firefly, "Drake's Orb" promises to take readers on a pulse-pounding adventure filled with action, suspense, and unexpected twists.

"Drake's Orb" is now available on [list the platforms where the book can be purchased, e.g., Amazon, Barnes & Noble, etc.]. Readers can also visit [your website or author platform] for more information and updates.

About the Author:
[Your Name] is an accomplished author known for their unique blend of thrilling storytelling and rich character development. With a passion for science fiction, they continue to captivate readers with their imaginative worlds and thought-provoking narratives.

For media inquiries, interviews, or review copies, please contact:

[Your Name]
[Your Email Address]
[Your Phone Number]

Note: Customize the press release by adding specific details about your book, such as its word count, format, genre, and any notable accolades or endorsements. Also, include quotes or reviews from advance readers, if available.

Although some authors will not use a press release, this is a useful tool to keep on hand if the opportunity arises and a newspaper, magazine, website, or other media entity becomes part of your book launch.

Book promotion is a crucial aspect of an author's success, and sometimes it can feel like a daunting task. However, by utilizing ChatGPT's features, we can identify our target audience, craft compelling book blurbs, create effective marketing materials and identify promotion opportunities. With these tools, we can take the steps needed to successfully launch our books, take our efforts to the next level and reach a wider audience.

One final benefit I've found in using ChatGPT for promotions is having it give me a hand up in creating Amazon ads. The process is pretty much the same for each book, depending on the genre, but having a step by step guide to ad creation has proven to be a most useful tool. There are always adjustments and tweaks to work on later, but for a quick guide, it does the trick. Below is the prompt and result I got from ChatGPT. To make it more interesting, I asked it to create an Amazon Marketing Campaign for my SciFi novel Drake's Orb using the process I wrote down for my Urban Fantasy novel Connections In Crimson:

Q: The following is an Amazon Marketing Campaign for the urban fantasy novel Connections In Crimson. Using the setup below as a template, provide a campaign for the scifi novel Drake's Orb by Alex G Zarate

Amazon Marketing Campaign

Step 1
Log into your kdp account
https://kdp.amazon.com/en_US/bookshelf

Step 2
Select "Marketing" from the menu at the top

Step 3
Under "Amazon Advertising", select "choose a market place", then "Amazon.com", then "Create a Campaign"

Step 4
Select "Sponsored Products", and press continue

Step5
Campaign name:
"Connections– SP1"
This stands for "Connections in Crimson" – Sponsored Product 1

Step 6
Start: Select your preferred starting date, or just leave it as it is (recommended because then it will immediately start)
You can always deactivate or pause the campaign later.

Step 7
Daily budget
Minimum of $1, which I would also start with.
Again this does not mean that the money WILL be used. You only pay when someone clicks on your book's ad and is directed to your book's page. When the campaign becomes starts to show fruition, you can always up the budget to increase exposure!

Step 8
Targeting
Select "Manual Targeting"

Step 9
Campaign Bidding Strategy
Select "Dynamic bids – up and down" for now. If you want to give Amazon a little more freedom, then select "up and down" as this will help you get more exposure.

Step 10
Ad Format
Select "Custom Text Ad"

Step 11
Products
Select your book/s by clicking the "Ad" button next to it. I would recommend selecting every version of your book.

Step 12
Targeting
Select "Keywords Targeting"

Step 13
Bid
Select "Custom Bid" and set the bidding to $0.49 for now.

Step 14
Match Type
Select only "Broad" and deselect "Phrase" and "exact"

Step 15
Keyword Targeting
Click on "Enter List"
Copy and paste the list of keywords below:
(These you change directly through your KDP Bookshelf for each book.)
1.   fiction book about teleportation
2.   science fiction about coming of age
3.   supernatural crime book about animals

4.   *unexpected mysterious discovery*
5.   *fighting to survive suspense fiction*
6.   *coming of age suspense fantasy*
7.   *fantasy book about premonition*

Click on "Add Keywords"
Ignore the words that are left over after you have clicked "add".

Step 16
Negative Keyword Targeting
Skip this step

Step 17
Creative
In the "Custom Text" box, copy paste the following text:
Option 1
A supernatural suspense book about a young man gifted with the ability to see thoughts and teleport by his cat, other humans with magical abilities, and a nightmare that could destroy the world!

Dark fantasy meets teen fiction in this bloodsucking novel about vampires, mythical creatures, paranormal romances and dreadfully dark secrets! Beware the damned!

Suspense meets mystery in this book about waking up in blood after a wild night out, a mysterious encounter with strangers, and a dead best friend.

Step 18
Launch Campaign!

A:
Amazon Marketing Campaign for Drake's Orb by Alex G Zarate

Step 1 Log into your KDP account
https://kdp.amazon.com/en_US/bookshelf

Step 2 Select "Marketing" from the menu at the top

Step 3 Under "Amazon Advertising", select "choose a marketplace", then "Amazon.com", then "Create a Campaign"

Step 4 Select "Sponsored Products", and press continue

Step 5 Campaign Name: "Drake's Orb – SP1"
This stands for "Drake's Orb" – Sponsored Product 1

Step 6 Start: Select your preferred starting date, or just leave it as it is (recommended because then it will immediately start) You can always deactivate or pause the campaign later.

Step 7 Daily Budget Minimum of $1, which I would also start with. Again this does not mean that the money WILL be used. You only pay when someone clicks on your book's ad and is directed to your book's page. When the campaign starts to show fruition, you can always up the budget to increase exposure!

Step 8 Targeting Select "Manual Targeting"

Step 9 Campaign Bidding Strategy Select "Dynamic bids – up and down" for now. If you want to give Amazon a little more freedom, then select "up and down" as this will help you get more exposure.

Step 10 Ad Format Select "Custom Text Ad"

Step 11 Products Select your books by clicking the "Ad" button next to it. I would recommend selecting every version of your book.

Step 12 Targeting Select "Keyword Targeting"

Step 13 Bid Select "Custom Bid" and set the bidding to $0.49 for now.

Step 14 Match Type Select only "Broad" and deselect "Phrase" and "exact"

Step 15 Keyword Targeting Click on "Enter List" Copy and paste the list of keywords below:

sci-fi adventure novel
space exploration fiction
first contact sci-fi
sci-fi book about time travel
interstellar space adventure
technology and humanity in sci-fi
action-packed space opera

Click on "Add Keywords" Ignore the words that are left over after you have clicked "add".

Step 16 Negative Keyword Targeting Skip this step

Step 17 Creative In the "Custom Text Ad" box, copy paste the following text:

Option 1 Embark on a thrilling adventure through time and space in the sci-fi epic, Drake's Orb. Join the journey of a team of explorers as they make contact with alien civilizations and uncover the secrets of a mysterious orb.

Option 2 Dive into a world of interstellar space exploration in the sci-fi novel, Drake's Orb. Follow the story of a team of daring adventurers as they encounter alien species and grapple with the consequences of their discovery.

Step 18 Launch Campaign!

As you can see, there are few corrections to be made but overall, it is an excellent guide for ad creation. Since I write across several genres, this has proven to be an excellent way of keeping each ad campaign on track as I prep one series after another.

May we all embrace the transformative power of ChatGPT in our book promotions, and watch as the burden of every book launch is lifted. This remarkable tool serves as a guiding light, providing an organized and seamless process that helps pave the way to literary success.

As you take each step forward, what may have once appeared daunting will become a manageable journey, laying the foundation for years to come. Trust in your abilities, passions and tools. Let ChatGPT be your steadfast companion on the path to enduring success in the rewarding world of publishing.

10
TRANSLATION
How ChatGPT Can Help You Reach A Global Audience

One of the hardest tasks when sharing a novel, short story or article to a wide audience is rewriting it to a different language. Translation is a complex task, requiring knowledge of the chosen language, cultural nuances and conveying the intended meaning. My first book of photography and motivation was so successful, I felt the need to translate it to Spanish. Google Translate was a good start, but, as we soon discover while taking on a new challenge, more is required.

The following was the prompt I used for translating the blurb for Zarate Zen - Captured Images From My Life To Yours:

Q: Translate the following book blurb into fluent Spanish, maintaining the meaning and content:

If you are interested in nature photography and are looking for hopeful messages and positive words, then this is the perfect book for you!

Zarate Zen- Captured Images From My Life To Yours is uniquely designed to provide you with encouraging words and truly remarkable images captured over the years.

It is both a photography book and a book bursting with positive words, hopeful comments and daily affirmations.

Alex G Zarate has brilliantly crafted a superb book filled with beautiful images and words which will uplift and motivate you. He is a landscape and nature photographer who has been posting online for several years.

Whether you're interested in nature photography, are seeking a positive outlook for the world or know someone who is, this book will be the perfect companion!

Onwards! +

And here is the translation provided by ChatGPT:

A: Te interesa la fotografía de naturaleza? ¿Estás buscando mensajes esperanzadores y palabras positivas? ¡Entonces este es el libro perfecto para ti!

Zarate Zen: imágenes capturadas de mi vida a la tuya está diseñado exclusivamente para brindarte palabras de aliento e imágenes verdaderamente notables capturadas a lo largo de los años.

Es a la vez un libro de fotografía y un libro lleno de palabras positivas, comentarios esperanzadores y afirmaciones diarias.

Alex G Zarate ha elaborado de manera brillante un magnífico libro lleno de bellas imágenes y palabras que te animarán y motivarán. Es un fotógrafo de paisajes y naturaleza que ha estado publicando en línea durante varios años.

Ya sea que esté interesado en la fotografía de la naturaleza, esté buscando una perspectiva positiva del mundo o conozca a alguien que lo esté... este libro será el compañero perfecto.

¡Adelante! +

Once the book was complete, I wanted to trust unconditionally what was on the page, but I still sent it to a professional translator so I could have it checked for clarity. It came out very well and the translator only made some minor adjustments. Overall, it could have stood as is, but like many things, a critical eye can make all the difference.

Although I only used ChatGPT for a Spanish translation, there are many languages available at its disposal. I was surprised to see the list that ChatGPT gave me when I asked what it could translate. The following are the ones ChatGPT listed at the time I published this book:

Q: What languages can you translate from English with confidence and accuracy?

A: As an AI language model, I have the capability to translate English into several languages. Some of the languages I can translate English into include:

Spanish
French
German
Italian
Portuguese
Dutch
Russian
Chinese (Simplified and Traditional)
Japanese
Korean
Arabic
Hindi
Swedish
Norwegian
Danish
Polish
Finnish
Greek
Turkish
Hebrew
Indonesian
Thai
Vietnamese
Czech
Romanian
Hungarian
Ukrainian
Catalan
Bulgarian
Lithuanian

Please note that while I can provide translations, the quality of the translation may vary depending on the language pair and the complexity of the text.

My experience with the translation to Spanish has been positive so far. As with everything else, when utilizing ChatGPT for translation, confirming results can save revising time later.

As an exercise, I went online and found the original text to The Illiad. I copied a bit and asked ChatGPT for a translation.

Q: Please translate the following into English. Explain the meaning and significance of the excerpt as well:

μῆνιν ἄειδε θεὰ Πηληϊάδεω Ἀχιλῆος
οὐλομένην, ἣ μυρί' Ἀχαιοῖς ἄλγε' ἔθηκε,
πολλὰς δ' ἰφθίμους ψυχὰς Ἄϊδι προΐαψεν
ἡρώων, αὐτοὺς δὲ ἑλώρια τεῦχε κύνεσσιν
5οἰωνοῖσί τε πᾶσι, Διὸς δ' ἐτελείετο βουλή,
ἐξ οὗ δὴ τὰ πρῶτα διαστήτην ἐρίσαντε
Ἀτρεΐδης τε ἄναξ ἀνδρῶν καὶ δῖος Ἀχιλλεύς.
τίς τ' ἄρ σφωε θεῶν ἔριδι ξυνέηκε μάχεσθαι;
Λητοῦς καὶ Διὸς υἱός: ὃ γὰρ βασιλῆϊ χολωθεὶς
10νοῦσον ἀνὰ στρατὸν ὄρσε κακήν, ὀλέκοντο δὲ λαοί,
οὕνεκα τὸν Χρύσην ἠτίμασεν ἀρητῆρα
Ἀτρεΐδης: ὃ γὰρ ἦλθε θοὰς ἐπὶ νῆας Ἀχαιῶν
λυσόμενός τε θύγατρα φέρων τ' ἀπερείσι' ἄποινα,
στέμματ' ἔχων ἐν χερσὶν ἑκηβόλου Ἀπόλλωνος
15χρυσέῳ ἀνὰ σκήπτρῳ, καὶ λίσσετο πάντας Ἀχαιούς,
Ἀτρεΐδα δὲ μάλιστα δύω, κοσμήτορε λαῶν:
Ἀτρεΐδαι τε καὶ ἄλλοι ἐϋκνήμιδες Ἀχαιοί,
ὑμῖν μὲν θεοὶ δοῖεν Ὀλύμπια δώματ' ἔχοντες
ἐκπέρσαι Πριάμοιο πόλιν, εὖ δ' οἴκαδ' ἱκέσθαι:
20παῖδα δ' ἐμοὶ λύσαιτε φίλην, τὰ δ' ἄποινα δέχεσθαι,
ἁζόμενοι Διὸς υἱὸν ἑκηβόλον Ἀπόλλωνα.

Although not a direct translation, the information provided is very useful and worth considering. If I were writing an article on The Illiad or researching a paper and wanted to use the original text for more data, this method would be essential. Give it a try with different languages, different texts or use your own prompts. The sky's the limit!

An interesting prompt that can be used is one I composed for cross/genre-purposes. I wanted to see if it were possible to have ChatGPT take one genre and convert it into another. See below:

Q: I want you to act as a Genre Translator. I will provide an entry and you will detect the meaning, translate it into the new genre version of text. Replace each sentence with the most easily recognizable genre version words and sentences. Maintain the meaning but make them more literarily apt. Translate the following Romance excerpt into a Suspense Thriller:

An awkward silence fell upon us, stretching for what felt like an eternity. After ten long minutes, he finally broke the silence with a question that caught me off guard. His gaze locked with mine momentarily before I shifted my focus to the captivating scenery outside, deliberately avoiding his striking features.

"Jazz," I replied softly, almost in a whisper. To my astonishment, the notes of one of my favorite jazz pieces began to fill the air, seemingly conjured by some unseen force.

"How are you acquainted with Jasmine?" he inquired, his voice so close it felt as if he were whispering into my ear, despite being on the other side of the limousine.

A: A heavy, tense silence descended upon us, stretching like a coiled wire, ready to snap at any moment. The passing minutes dragged on, each tick of the clock increasing the unease, until finally, he shattered the suffocating stillness with a sudden and unexpected question, causing my heart to skip a beat. Our eyes locked for a fleeting instant, a silent battle of wills, before I redirected my attention to the alluring landscape beyond, intentionally avoiding his captivating visage.

"Jazz," I murmured under my breath, my words barely audible, like a secret meant only for the wind. And then, to my bewildered amazement, the haunting melody of my beloved jazz composition swelled through the air, as if summoned by an elusive and enigmatic force.

"How do you know Jasmine?" he inquired, his voice a breath away, a sinister whisper that sent shivers down my spine, despite the physical barrier of the limousine that separated us.

Overall, the prompt worked well, and if modified, should work for most any genre. Interested in trying different genres? This may be the key.

As a writer, it is sometimes necessary to step into the shoes of someone we are unfamiliar with. This can be difficult if you are trying to write as someone in the military, a doctor, lawyer or a member of law enforcement. In these instances, it is useful to have ChatGPT help in phrasing things to fit the character, scenario or scene.

Q: For a detective novel set in present-day New York, translate the following excerpt into a format that would be used in an official police report: Johnathan Doe was walking past his next-door neighbor's house when he heard a scream. He heard a gunshot and called the police as he ran to the door of the house. He saw his neighbor running out the back door and was about to go after him when he heard a voice from inside the house and walked in, finding his wife on the ground, wounded. He remained with her until emergency services arrived.

A:
Date: [Date of Incident]
Time: [Time of Incident]
Location: [Address of Incident]

Incident Report

Reporting Officer: [Your Name]
Badge Number: [Your Badge Number]

Incident Details:

On [Date of Incident], at approximately [Time of Incident], I, Officer [Your Name], responded to a distress call regarding a possible shooting at [Address of Incident], New York.

Witness Information:

Witness: Johnathan Doe
Date of Birth: [Date of Birth]
Phone Number: [Witness's Phone Number]

Statement:

According to Mr. Doe's statement, he was walking past his next-door neighbor's house when he heard a scream followed by the sound of a gunshot. In response to the suspicious noises, he immediately contacted the police while heading towards the front door of the residence.

Mr. Doe reported seeing his neighbor fleeing through the back door. However, his attention was diverted when he heard a voice coming from inside the house. Acting with caution, he entered the property and discovered his wife lying on the ground, visibly injured.

Actions Taken:

Mr. Doe remained with his wounded wife, providing aid and comfort, until emergency services arrived at the scene.

Injuries and Damages:

•   Mrs. Doe was found wounded on the ground inside the residence.

Request for Assistance:

Additional officers and medical personnel were dispatched to the scene to secure the area and attend to the injured.

Further Investigation:

Upon arrival, I observed the crime scene and secured the area for further investigation by the Detective Division.

Conclusion:

The situation is under investigation, and further actions will be taken as necessary to determine the circumstances surrounding the incident.

Witness Signature: ______________________________
Officer Signature: ______________________________

End of Report

Adding an air of authenticity can go a long way to make your story come alive. This also gives the reader a glimpse into the worlds we write about.

Q: Provide the proper verbiage for the following that would be used by a veteran paramedic as he calls in to the hospital: "I am transporting a wounded woman in her twenties who has a gunshot wound to her upper chest between her shoulder and collar bone. There has been significant blood loss and a trauma surgeon needs to be available upon arrival."

A:
Dispatch: [Hospital Name], this is Paramedic [Your Name] with Unit [Unit Number].

Hospital: Go ahead, [Unit Number].

Dispatch: We are en route to your location with a wounded female patient in her twenties. The patient sustained a gunshot wound to her upper chest, located between her shoulder and collar bone. Significant blood loss has occurred, and we require a trauma surgeon to be prepared for immediate intervention upon our arrival.

Hospital: Copy that, [Unit Number]. We will notify the trauma team and prepare for the patient's arrival. ETA?

Dispatch: Approximately [Estimated Time of Arrival].

Hospital: Understood, [Unit Number]. We'll be ready to receive the patient. Safe travels.

Dispatch: Thank you, [Hospital Name]. See you soon. [Unit Number] out.

As you can see, the subtleties involved in each role are significant when you take into consideration what the characters must say in their jobs. No matter where you go, you will discover people and jobs develop their own lingo. Use ChatGPT to break the language gap.

You can also have ChatGPT give you a completely fabricated word, phrase or language to incorporate into your story:

Q: You are the translator of a made-up language set in a fantasy world populated by glowing beings who have bird-like qualities including the ability to fly. I will provide you with a sentence and you will translate it to this new language. My first sentence is: "Hello, I'm Bob, from another world. Who are you?"

A: In the made-up language of the glowing beings with bird-like qualities, the translation of the provided sentence would be:

"Sulerei, ilumë Bob, renna ulae nirindar. Síra andorë ya'alei?"

Please note that this translation is purely fictional, as per the parameters you have described. It captures the essence of the given sentence in a way that aligns with the fantasy world you have described.

When creating fictional worlds, science fiction societies, secret societies or fantasy realms, ChatGPT can become a great tool. For example: Need help with translating Klingon?

Q: You are fluent in the Klingon language from Star Trek and can translate from English to Klingon or Klingon to English. Translate the following into Klingon, including pronunciation guide: "I will succeed in making my dreams a reality and claim my passions with honor and glory."

A: "I will succeed in making my dreams a reality and claim my passions with honor and glory" can be translated into Klingon as:

"jIyajbe'chugh, HIq vI'el DIlmoH, 'ej jagh vItlhutlh."

Pronunciation guide:

jIyajbe'chugh: jee-yahj-beh-chookh
HIq: heek
vI'el: vee-ehl
DIlmoH: deel-mokh
'ej: ej (short and quick)
jagh: jahgh
vItlhutlh: vitlh-ootlh (oo as in "boot")

Please note that Klingon is a constructed language, and while efforts have been made to create a consistent grammar and vocabulary, there may be variations in translations. The pronunciation guide provided here is an approximation based on established phonetic guidelines.

Unlock the boundless potential of ChatGPT as a translation tool to enrich your Sci-Fi universe, infuse enchanting fantasy cultures with new dimensions or delve deeper into the marvels of languages that surround us.

With ChatGPT as your linguistic ally, you'll be amazed at the horizons it unlocks, breathing life into new worlds and propelling your creative endeavors to unprecedented heights. Embrace the magic of translation and let your imagination soar like never before.

CONCLUSION

CONCLUSIONS AND COVER QUESTIONS

Remember: The questions I've posed to ChatGPT throughout the book are mere examples. They might not the best questions to ask or the best phrased prompts for your specific needs. Use them as guideposts. Take what I have shared as a launchpad to your own writing. Whatever needs you have in your stories, articles or novels, use ChatGPT to attain greater results.

ONE MORE THING...

Although the following prompts are not writing related, I wanted to include them as they've proven useful in my needs as a novelist. After all, getting the best cover design for our publication is a part of the process.

The cover design of a book is often the first impression that potential readers have of our book. A great cover can attract readers as well as convey the genre and tone of the book. It can also influence purchasing decisions. To start off, let's ask a general question:

Q: I want to create a cover design for my novel. What should I know moving forward?

A: Creating a cover design for your novel is an exciting and important step in the publishing process. Here are some key points to consider as you move forward:

1. Visualize Your Concept: Start by visualizing the theme, tone, and essence of your novel. Consider the main elements, characters, or settings that represent the core of your story. Think about the emotions you want to evoke in your potential readers.

2. Research Market Trends: Look at book covers in your genre to get an idea of current market trends and what attracts readers in your niche. Note the colors, fonts, and imagery commonly used in successful covers.

3. Professional Design or DIY: Decide whether you want to hire a professional cover designer or create the design yourself. While a professional designer can ensure a polished and eye-catching cover, there are also DIY tools and templates available for authors on a budget.

4. Eye-Catching Typography: Choose fonts that are legible and visually appealing. The title should be clear and easy to read, even in thumbnail size. Consider using custom typography to make your cover stand out.

5. High-Quality Imagery: If you include images or illustrations, make sure they are of high resolution and fit the genre and theme of your novel. Avoid using low-quality or generic stock images.

6. Cohesive Design: Ensure that the elements of your cover, such as images, fonts, and colors, work together cohesively. The cover should convey a unified message and capture the essence of your story.

7. Size and Format: Design your cover in the appropriate dimensions for both print and digital formats. Print covers require higher resolution, while digital covers should be optimized for online platforms.

8. Test with Your Audience: Once you have a design, gather feedback from your target audience or beta readers. Their input can help you fine-tune the cover and make sure it resonates with potential readers.

9. Back Cover and Spine: Don't forget to design the back cover and spine for print editions. The back cover should include a captivating blurb, author bio, and any endorsements or reviews.

10. Copyright and Permissions: Ensure that you have the right to use any images or elements in your cover design. If you hire a designer or use stock images, make sure you have the necessary permissions and licenses.

Remember that your book cover is the first impression readers will have of your novel. A well-designed cover can grab attention, spark interest, and entice potential readers to pick up your book. Take your time in the design process, and don't hesitate to seek professional help if needed.

The advice given seems to be geared for those who are making their own cover designs. This is one of the methods I used when starting and still use for some of my books today. An additional question to pose for developing our own covers can be:

Q: What free or inexpensive tools are available for book cover designing?

A: There are several free or inexpensive tools available for book cover designing that can help you create a professional-looking cover. Here are some popular options:

1. Canva: Canva is a user-friendly graphic design platform with a vast library of templates and elements. While some premium elements may require payment, there are plenty of free resources to create a stunning book cover.

2. GIMP: GIMP (GNU Image Manipulation Program) is a free and open-source raster graphics editor. It offers powerful features similar to Adobe Photoshop and can be used for creating book covers.

3. Pixlr: Pixlr is an online photo editing tool that offers a range of features, including layers and filters. It has a free version with ads or a premium version with additional features.

4.   Adobe Spark: Adobe Spark provides templates for book covers, and you can customize them to suit your needs. It has a free plan with limited features, as well as premium options.

5.   BookBrush: BookBrush is a specialized book cover design tool that offers a free plan with limited access to templates and elements. There are also affordable premium plans with more options.

6.   Cover Design Studio: This online tool allows you to create book covers using their templates and customization options. It has both free and premium elements available.

7.   DIY Book Covers: DIY Book Covers is a website that offers free templates for book covers. It allows you to create basic covers quickly and easily.

8. Snappa: Snappa offers a variety of design templates, including book covers. It has a free version with limited downloads and a premium plan for more features.

Remember that while these tools can help you create a book cover on a budget, design expertise and a keen eye for aesthetics can make a significant difference. If you're unsure about your design skills, consider seeking feedback from others or hiring a professional cover designer to ensure your book cover looks polished and appealing.

I've used GIMP before and liked the results. As a free Photoshop substitute, it's amazing! Also, BookBrush is a current fave. It has an option to design your covers with page count taken into consideration as well as customization options for paperback, hard cover or ebook variations. (The mock-up feature is also worth checking out) Try them all or look for more until you find the right one for you. Like ChatGPT, there are amazing tools out there just waiting to be discovered!

If you choose to hire a professional for your cover design needs, keep in mind the criteria that ChatGPT listed. If you are unfamiliar with the specific Genre needs for each book cover, ChatGPT can help narrow down the specifics:

Q: I need help designing a book cover. Please provide a detailed list of Genre-specific design tips I can take into consideration.

A: Designing a book cover that resonates with readers in your specific genre is crucial for attracting the right audience. Here are some detailed genre-specific design tips to consider:

1. Romance:

•   Emphasize emotions: Use images or colors that convey love, passion, or tenderness.
•   Couples and embraces: Include images of couples, close-ups of hands, or embraces to evoke romantic feelings.
•   Soft color palette: Pastel or warm colors often work well for romance covers.
•   Whimsical fonts: Consider using elegant and flowing fonts to match the romantic theme.

2. Mystery/Thriller:

•   Dark and mysterious: Employ a dark or moody color scheme to create suspense.
•   Intriguing visuals: Use symbolic images or objects related to the plot to pique readers' curiosity.
•   Bold fonts: Choose bold and sharp fonts to create a sense of urgency and tension.

3. Science Fiction:

•   Futuristic elements: Incorporate futuristic technology or settings to set the sci-fi tone.

• *Cosmic or otherworldly backgrounds: Use space images or otherworldly landscapes to create a sense of wonder.*
• *Modern and sleek fonts: Opt for modern and clean fonts that reflect the sci-fi genre.*

4. *Fantasy:*

• *Magical elements: Include magical symbols, creatures, or enchanted objects to evoke a sense of wonder.*
• *Ethereal and dreamy: Use soft, dreamlike colors and imagery to create a fantastical atmosphere.*
• *Decorative fonts: Choose ornate and fantasy-inspired fonts that match the mystical theme.*

5. *Historical Fiction:*

• *Vintage aesthetics: Utilize sepia tones or faded colors to evoke a historical feel.*
• *Period-appropriate visuals: Include images that represent the time period and setting of the story.*
• *Classic and elegant fonts: Opt for fonts that reflect the era or are reminiscent of historical writing.*

6. *Young Adult:*

• *Vibrant and dynamic: Use bold colors and energetic imagery to appeal to a youthful audience.*
• *Youthful protagonists: Feature young characters or symbols that represent adolescence.*
• *Playful and modern fonts: Consider using contemporary fonts that resonate with a young audience.*

7. *Children's:*

• *Use bright colors and bold, playful graphics that will appeal to children.*

*   Use a clear and legible font for the title and author name, and make sure the title is prominent.
*   Use simple, eye-catching designs that will stand out in a crowded market.

8.   Non-Fiction (Self-Help):

*   Inspirational images: Include uplifting or motivational visuals that align with the book's theme.
*   Minimalistic design: Emphasize simplicity and clarity to convey a sense of guidance.
*   Clean and professional fonts: Choose clear and readable fonts that communicate authority.

Remember, while these genre-specific tips can be helpful, it's essential to understand your target audience and the specific themes of your book to create a cover that effectively represents your story and captures readers' attention. Consider seeking feedback from others, especially from your target audience, to ensure your book cover resonates with potential readers.

Each of these are worth keeping in mind when designing a cover or when requesting a cover design from a professional. For example:

Q: I am submitting a Science Fiction cover design request to a professional service. From the description below, provide the most effective submission for the best results:

I want the cover design to be the captain standing by his first officer in a large room with the stars visible through the far wall. The captain has dark hair, clean shaven and in scifi armor. His first officer is a blonde woman also in armor and neither are wearing a helmet.

A: Title: Galactic Odyssey

Description:
For the cover design, I envision a compelling scene that captures the essence of the story. The backdrop should be a large, futuristic spacecraft room with a sleek, transparent wall revealing the vast expanse of stars and galaxies beyond. The lighting inside the room should be dim, casting dramatic shadows and creating an atmosphere of mystery and adventure.

At the center of the design, I want the protagonist, Captain Johnathan Drake, depicted in his sci-fi armor. He has dark, slicked-back hair and a clean-shaven face, exuding a sense of determination and authority. His armor should look sleek, with glowing elements to highlight its advanced technology.

Standing alongside Captain Drake is his trusted first officer, Lieutenant Amelia West. She is a confident and skilled woman with flowing blonde hair and a strong presence. Like the captain, she is dressed in sci-fi armor that accentuates her prowess and readiness for action.

Both characters should be portrayed without helmets, showcasing their faces and expressions. Their eyes should reflect a sense of camaraderie, trust, and an unyielding spirit as they face the unknown challenges of space exploration.

The overall style of the cover design should be visually stunning, with attention to detail and a touch of cinematic flair. The use of vibrant colors for the sci-fi elements will contrast beautifully against the dark backdrop of the stars, adding depth and visual appeal.

The title "Galactic Odyssey" should be bold and prominent, positioned at the top or bottom of the cover in a modern, sci-fi-inspired font that complements the overall design.

I am open to the artist's creative interpretation and expertise in bringing this dynamic scene to life. The goal is to captivate readers with an eye-catching cover that embodies the spirit of adventure, exploration, and the bond between the captain and his first officer.

I did not provide the title to the book or named my characters (My bad) but overall, the result was excellent. When employing a cover design professional, it's important to give as much information as possible to get the best results.

A book's cover design is a critical component of its success, and ChatGPT offers several features to help authors design compelling and effective covers. By following general design guidelines and genre-specific conventions, authors can create a cover that attracts readers and accurately reflects the genre and tone of the book. Whether you're a novice author or a seasoned professional, ChatGPT's features can help you design a cover that will make a strong first impression and encourage readers to pick up your book.

Remember: ChatGPT is an AI language model and not a replacement for creativity or imagination. While it can provide inspiration and guidance, it's up to us to take the ideas generated by ChatGPT and turn them into something unique and original. By embracing the unexpected and using ChatGPT as a tool rather than a crutch, we can expand our creativity and take our writing to new and exciting places.

Onwards! +

Thank you for embarking on this writing journey with me in The Ultimate Guide To Writing With Chat GPT!

As you've journeyed through these pages, you've become a vital part of this adventure and I want to express my heartfelt gratitude for joining me. Just like my experiences in capturing images, writing has become a way for me to appreciate the wonders of the world. Each sentence has allowed me to see the beauty in every moment, every idea and every unique perspective that comes our way.

Through this guide, we've delved into storytelling and explored realms of creativity. I hope that this new tool will ignite a spark within you, inspiring your pen to dance across the page with renewed enthusiasm. As we move forward, let's remember that every day offers a fresh canvas for our creativity. Just like a breathtaking sunset or the flight of a majestic bird, there is magic in every word we pen and every tale we craft. Embrace the journey, relish the challenges, and celebrate the triumphs of our writing endeavors.

May this guide encourage you to embrace the beauty around you, to find inspiration in unexpected places, and to discover the extraordinary within yourself. As you continue your writing voyage, always remember that you possess the power to create worlds, touch hearts and leave an indelible mark on the tapestry of the world.

Thank you for being a part of this journey and may our writing adventures be filled with boundless joy, endless creativity, and the ever-inspiring beauty of the written word.

Onwards! +

WANT MORE?

Thank you again for sharing your time with me.
Please leave a rating, review and/or comment.

If you enjoyed this book,
I hope you will check out my other works.

Urban Fantasy/Supernatural Suspense:
Linked
Ripples of Mind
Echoes of Innocence
Connections In Crimson
Reflections In Darkness
Tremors In Time

Science Fiction:
Drake's Orb

Non-Fiction:
Zarate Zen: Captured Images From My Life To Yours
Zarate Zen: Colorful Captures & Positive Posts

The Ultimate Guide to Writing With Chat GPT: Harness The Power
Of Chat GPT To Write Smarter, Not Harder

Be well, my friends.

Onwards! +

ABOUT THE AUTHOR

Meet Alex G Zarate, a passionate writer, artist, and photographer, whose journey of creativity has led to the creation of The Ultimate Guide To Writing With Chat GPT. With a heart filled with wonder and a soul eager to explore new horizons, Alex has embarked on a quest to capture the beauty of life through words and imagery.

From an early age, Alex found solace and inspiration in the act of creation. The love for storytelling, like a spark, ignited a fervent desire to share captivating tales that transport readers to distant worlds and untold adventures. Through the lens of a camera, Alex discovered the art of freezing moments in time, preserving the essence of fleeting beauty for eternity.

As an author, Alex's writing resonates with authenticity and a deep understanding of human emotions. Each word is carefully chosen to weave a tapestry of emotion, connecting readers to the core of the narrative. From poetry to prose, Alex's works touch the hearts of those who embark on the literary journey.

Beyond the written word, Alex's artistic talent extends to captivating visuals. Each stroke of the brush or click of the shutter captures the essence of nature, showcasing the beauty that surrounds us all.

The Ultimate Guide To Writing With Chat GPT stands as a testament to Alex's passion for creativity and a profound belief in the transformative power of language. With an unwavering dedication to the craft of storytelling, Alex seeks to inspire others to embrace their creative potential. As a guide and mentor, Alex's nurturing spirit encourages writers to break free from limitations and explore the boundless possibilities of their imagination.

In The Ultimate Guide To Writing With Chat GPT, Alex invites readers on a remarkable journey, guiding them through the art of writing with a language model, and opening doors to endless realms of creativity.

With a heart brimming with enthusiasm and a mind filled with dreams, Alex G Zarate continues to explore the wonders of storytelling, art, and photography. Embrace the journey of creativity and join Alex in discovering the beauty and magic that lies within us all.

Onwards! +

You can find him online at: www.alexgzarate.com

Or on social media at:
TWITTER: twitter.com/zaratecreations
FACEBOOK: facebook.com/alexgzarate
INSTAGRAM: instagram.com/alexgzarate
YOUTUBE: youtube.com/alexgzarate

Or search online for Alex G Zarate. You'll find him.

www.ingramcontent.com/pod-product-compliance
Lightning Source LLC
Chambersburg PA
CBHW070519160726
48003CB00004B/1632